Y0-BGT-804

A New England Autumn

A New England Autumn

80 color photographs by Gerd Kittel

Introduction by Eleanor Munro

Thames and Hudson

ACKNOWLEDGMENTS

For help and support I would like to thank Stanley Baron and Wolfgang Keller. I am also indebted to the firm Lufthansa A.G.

Gerd Kittel

Any copy of this book issued by the publisher as a paperback is sold subject to the condition that it shall not by way of trade or otherwise be lent, resold, hired out of otherwise circulated without the publisher's prior consent in any form of binding or cover other than that in which it is published and without a similar condition including these words being imposed on a subsequent purchaser.

Photographs and captions © 1987 Gerd Kittel
Introduction © 1987 Eleanor Munro

First published in the United States in 1987 by Thames and Hudson Inc., 500 Fifth Avenue, New York, New York 10110

Library of Congress Catalog Card Number 87-50186

All Rights Reserved. No part of this publication may be reproduced or transmitted in any form or by any means, electronic or mechanical, including photocopy, recording or any other information storage and retrieval system, without prior permission in writing from the publisher.

Printed and bound in Japan by Dai Nippon

Contents

Introduction 7

Captions to the plates 19

The Plates 25

Erst hört man von Natur und Nachahmung derselben; dann soll es eine schöne Natur geben. Man soll wählen. Doch wohl das Beste! Und woran soll man's erkennen? Nach welcher Norm soll man wählen? Und wo ist denn die Norm? Doch wohl nicht auch in der Natur?

. . . Es ist daher das Beste, wenn wir bei Beobachtungen so viel als möglich uns der Gegenstände und bei'm Denken darüber so viel als möglich uns unsrer selbst bewußt sind.

Johann Wolfgang Goethe

(We hear much about Nature, and about the imitation of Nature; but then there is also supposed to be a beautiful Nature. We are to select; and no doubt we are to select the best. But how are we meant to recognize it? What is to be our criterion? And where does the criterion reside? Surely not in Nature itself?

. . . It is therefore best, when observing, to be aware as much as possible of the object; and when reflecting upon it to be aware as much as possible of ourselves.)

Introduction

It seems strange, to one who has wandered many of the terrains so fascinatingly photographed by Gerd Kittel – woodlands, hills, salt-flats and villages, under various lights and weathers – , to see them so emptied of people. In that single respect, a number of these photographs belong in the tradition of nineteenth-century Edenic landscape paintings – of vast New England river valleys and sky-raking mountains – similarly emptied of human presence but replete with a luminous atmospheric glow representing a transcendental spirit-of-nature. The works at hand, however, are meticulously realistic, not mystical, and so promise to reveal at least an aspect of the "real" New England. So they do, but paradoxically. For real New Englanders, who feel for their landscape a fierce and down-to-earth affection, also tend to see it populated by layers upon layers of ghosts.

It would be, I think, a rare New Englander who, asked to describe the view from his or her front porch, wouldn't begin by summoning up ancestral figures of a century or so ago, those who cleared the fields of glacial rubble, piled up the grey-stone walls, sowed orchards and kitchen gardens, built churches, formulated and manned the town councils and boards of governors. Then that ruminative New Englander would call to mind departed friends who only yesterday ran the store, bred the cattle and put out to sea when the cod were running. And then at last you'd hear about the good neighbors who, just down the road and around the bend, perform these same homely chores today.

Now, it's true that physical isolation is considered a virtue here. Resident New Englanders express satisfaction in their distance from the fleshpots to the south and west. And vacationers prefer to follow our lonely byways, not the thruways, into our deep green summer or blazingly colored autumn forests. Likewise, many travelers head northeast to hike the unpopulated New England portion of the Adirondack Trail or to ski cross-country over virgin snowfields. But sooner or later, when their carburetor needs attention or they run out of mosquito balm or ski-wax, they'll happen by a hardware store on some remote turning, and before an hour has passed (transactions take place in their own time-frame here), they'll know as much about farmer Mooney's difficulties with his tomatoes and good Mary Kane's success with her beach plum jelly as those who've lived here for generations.

Therefore, I'm inspired by these curiously silent photos to summon back for conversation some of my own ghosts, perhaps settling ourselves for a while on Gerd Kittel's trio of chairs turned to a lake full of mist darkening into twilight – chairs exactly like those in my house now, on which certain of those who are now ghosts sat down in life.

For my life is enmeshed in New England and its geographical and cultural extension in northeastern New York State. Back when the Revolutionary guns sounded, one of my thrice-great grandfathers, Samuel Greeley Spaulding, though but a boy, took himself off to Fort Ticonderoga and, at least according to our family mythology, was standing next to Ethan Allen there when the British laid down their arms. A bit later, at last of age, he officially served in a New Hampshire regiment and so earned, for his descendants ever after, pride of connection with those great events.

When peace was made and he married, Spaulding determined to put down roots along the romantic and – save for friendly Indians – uninhabited shores of Lake Champlain. For in the Adirondack forests were profitable stands of hardwood and also streams and waterfalls to power mill wheels. Thus, in the year 1800, he entered the wilderness, hacked his way toward a high summit, which afforded a view of the Lake to the north, the Green Mountains of Vermont to the east and the Adirondacks to the west, and there staked his camp. Some forty families recruited from overpopulated Vermont and New Hampshire followed, each felling the necessary trees, burning off the fields and building a log cabin. Soon to the woodland crossroads came a store and also a school – like the one in photo 27 – where five small scholars sat on pine slabs to learn their lessons. And so from my pioneer ancestor's labor sprang the town now known as Crown Point.

In those days throughout New England and neighboring states, there was a simple living to be earned by selling potash, made from the ashes of trees being cleared. And in the winter, when people were housebound by snowdrifts high as the eaves, wooden articles like shingles, barrel staves, brooms, baskets and hay rakes could be whittled and joined for sale come spring in the prosperous villages of Vermont. And sap from the sugar maple trees – the indigenous American species that provides the gold-vermilion flush across New England in the fall – could be boiled down into marketable cakes. And before a half-century had unrolled, ore-smelting furnaces and iron works appeared among the mineral-rich hills, and there were spinning mills by the streams and inns for traveling merchants. And networks of canals and railways linked New England to the Great Lakes in the west, and what had been frontier was frontier no longer.

Such progress seemed wonderful to New Englanders of the time. As an old man, my Spaulding twice-great grandfather put his pen to paper thus: "When I meditate on the great change that has taken place since my remembrance, I become lost in wonder. It seems as though man had aspired to be a Deity. He has called the lightnings down from the clouds, harnessed them up and made them do the work of our post-boys. He has called down the Sunbeams and made them paint our pictures [he was thinking of course of the new science of photography]. He has analized [sic] the air, measured the depth of the ocean, and bound the earth in iron bands. With the same ratio of progress for the next century as in the past, he will have the essential power of nature under his control."

There comes then a break in my connection with the northeast but a crucial one for me. For a descendant of Samuel Greeley Spaulding, bored by the tameness of a town grown prosperous, packed his trunks – along with stores of seed packets of vegetables, fruit trees and flowers – and joined the Great Migration of New Englanders and others into the newly opened, barren and untreed prairies beyond the Mississippi. Out there, his daughter, who would become my grandmother, married an immigrant Scot, whose familial line went back to before Culloden (among the Hebridean Scots, immigration fever ran so high there was a dance – one of the few not forbidden the orthodox to join –

called "America", in which couples whirled in circles, one after another, till all were in motion). So my father was born on the Nebraska frontier to a daughter of New England, who shortly became nostalgic for cultural advantages, bundled up her baby and, with her Gaelic-speaking husband, rode the rails back toward the sunrise.

Though they didn't return to her birthplace, they remained New Englanders in spirit. They settled in the northern environs of Manhattan, in what was then still a sort of rural village community, with many trees and wood frame houses exactly like those in villages here photographed by Kittel. There my father grew up in a close-knit community of Anglo-Saxon churchgoers devoted to books and social improvement. Thus he was formed, although on the edge of a metropolis and on the cusp of the Modern age, according to the moral and cultural values of his Puritan forebears. And in time, he attended the famous Dutch-founded high school in Brooklyn, Erasmus Hall, one of the glories of the young American public education system, which churned several generations of European immigrants into a single citizenry speaking a single language, all of them to be, at least in literary taste, "New Englanders."

But my roots, at least in my fantasy, go back still farther, even to the time of discovery of the land-mass atop which New England would be an early implantation. For the proud and infinitely hopeful name given my Spaulding great-grandfather – the one who went west like Johnny Appleseed, taking along his daughter who would be my grandmother – was Americus Vespuccius. The first Amerigo Vespucci's expeditionary reports, as we know, inspired Sir Thomas More's *Utopia*, a text that contributed to what would become New England consciousness, or that part of it that can be summed up as cooperative trust in one's neighbor and confidence in the generally progressive destiny of humankind.

When he died at the age of 77 in Nebraska, Americus' obituary recounted his descent from a time when the nation was young and New England's political vision a fresh bud:

Up under the shadow of the Adirondack mountains is a good place in which to be born, for from those grand old hills started the springs of political power in Colonial days, flowing like rivulets from the north Ticonderoga, until the meeting of liberty's streams made possible Bunker Hill and Lexington. From his mother's breast, he drank in a love of liberty, and out of that primitive mountain home came a character founded on the unshaken rock of God's word.

Love of New England's mountains flowed on in my family's veins. Thus my father's parents, when they retired from their teaching professions, bought a cabin halfway up a steep slope some hundred miles north of Manhattan. To that house, from our own more urbane house in Ohio, we drove as a family every summer all the years of my childhood, packed into our old tin lizzie, rattling over the highways till we sighted a certain white church with pointed belfry. There we turned left and rushed on by it to a dirt road that wound up through the deep pine woods, alongside the cow pasture, the chicken farm, past the German retirement home, on up and up till we sighted, deep in flaming tiger-lilies, our grandparents' place "in the country."

There, evening after evening, nestled in my grandfather's lap, I prepared in solemn happiness to hear a story. He would reach out a long arm and slowly pluck from his enormous black teacher's desk, from among his Testaments and Psalms, his Homer, his Tennyson and Longfellow, his Emerson, Darwin and Herbert Spencer, a yellow tin box of licorice. Like rusty machinery, his hands would work off the lid – knobby farmer's hands they were, despite his learning. He would offer me one tiny aromatic square, then as slowly replace the lid and the box, lean back his head and shut his eyes to shuffle around in his voluminous memory. I would look up into the deep pleats of his throat and wriggle impatiently. "Soo soo," he would say, patting my arms and hair. "Settle down and listen." And he would begin, in his gravelly brogue, to play on the strings of my imagination, recounting the tales of Horatio at the Bridge and Leonidas at the Pass, of Mowgli and

Ab, and the boy who saved the burning ship, and also tales of sorrow and exile, of Rip van Winkle and the Dog of Flanders, and the noble Highland clans uprooted and set to wandering.

"You are so wise, Bappa," I said more than once. And he would correct me, "Remember the wise man who walked by the sea and picked up a stone.

"'This stone,' he said, 'is what I know,' and he threw it into the sea.

"'And the ocean,' he said, 'is what I do not know.'"

His ghost, deep, melancholy, realistic, and yet, for all that, still with hope for the human condition, walks with me when I walk on a New England beach today.

Times change, of course. Terrible events have left their scars on the world. Humanity's hopes ride not so high but are held back by caution. Yet in New England – to generalize, though not inaccurately – old humanistic values survive and draw successive waves of new immigrants, in this case those city dwellers I mentioned above, drawn by ties ancestral or ideological to come home "to the country" to reorient themselves and restore their balance.

I claim a corner of New England myself these days – Cape Cod. Here my husband and I live half of each year in a 150-year-old house on a grassy dune in the middle of a meadow that runs east toward the Atlantic and west toward the Bay. The sun rises in our bedroom windows and sets in the kitchen windows, traveling all day – as wise old Cape Cod architects always contrived unless there was a taller dune in the way – across the south flank of the house, warming the tiny parlors. Down the road lives farmer Mooney, and across the field Mary Kane boils down her beach plum jelly every autumn. We know the postmistress and the oysterman, the history of their ancestors and the faces of their descendants, and last year there came to our door one warm afternoon, on the arm of her solicitous nephew, a ninety-eight-year-old woman born in the traditional "borning room" of our house, come to take a last look at the home that had been her father's. Surely her ghost will stand with me, evenings, when I look out of my window to see the sunset turn the sky orange-rose and the gulls overhead wing companionably home.

So though homesteads in New England change hands with a frequency that might seem to belie the sense of continuity I've been talking about, for us the ghosts of gone residents live on where they felt at ease, not forgotten.

Looking at Gerd Kittel's photographs, however, I feel I've not yet come to grips with the powerfully idiosyncratic attitude they communicate. I haven't yet ferreted out how this artist from a new Germany, first trained as a medical doctor, sees my New England.

To begin with, the photographs make a sharp and unusual claim on the attention. I recognize the physical environs, yet without that stir of recognition one experiences in the presence of a familiar person. The waterside town I know, with its weekend boats tied to a pier by absent owners. I know the hotel dining room, as empty of life as if, between two ticks of the grandfather clock that doubtless stands in the nearby lobby, some cosmic anesthesia had gripped it. The harvested fields I know, with random dry corn stalks left standing by a farmer vanished from the scene. Other shots I know in the way one knows what one has seen a hundred times yet out of indolence or distaste simply not taken account of: barber and hairdressing saloons, all plastic and philodendrons; a tacky motel lobby.

Still others I recognize not from experience but most likely from movies on the theme of social dislocation: lower-middle-class small-town night shots made sinister by the flare of neon and sodium lights.

The point is, the eye that selected these shots is one of strikingly dispassionate accuracy. I doubt my ruminative New Englander could so effectively clear his field of projected feelings and gird himself against the exercise of the pathetic fallacy. By contrast, Kittel fixes a surgical gaze on the box-car abandoned on its siding, the shuttered barn, the rusted pump, the family manse vacated behind unkempt grass. And in the end, he convinces me of the esthetic neutrality of the artifacts of my local culture when they are stripped of all projected sentimentalities.

On the other hand, I note an amount of black in this collective study that is not to be accounted for by New England's face as I know it. For example, outside the hard outline of a street-light, the night is pitch, uninflected black. The autumn woods, only a little way back from the photographer's feet, suddenly darken, not into the haunted gloom of Hawthorne's or Melville's short stories and novels, but to an utter, absolute black, like the abyss in Jonathan Edward's sermons. Perhaps Kittel's perception of and engagement with this depth of shadow reveals, consciously or unconsciously, his intuition of metaphysical absolutes, albeit expressed in terms of the world's objective appearance.

Yet – and to me this is the most interesting aspect of his work – he demonstrates the restingness, that is, the moral neutrality, of the physical world when the human component is not in evidence and the observer has washed his hands of contaminating illusions: a post-Modern expression of trust, yet trust all the same, as well befits a portrait of today's New England.

Eleanor Munro

Captions to the plates

 1. Lake Winnipesaukee, Melvin Village, New Hampshire
 2, 3. Lake Winnipesaukee, Wolfeboro, New Hampshire
 4. Crystal Lake, Connecticut
 5-7. Kancamagus Pass, White Mountain National Forest, New Hampshire
 8. Acadia National Park, Maine
 9. Near Brookton, Maine
 10. Kancamagus Pass
 11. Near Lincoln, White Mountain National Forest, New Hampshire
 12, 13. Near Chelsea, Vermont
 14. Near Goshen, Connecticut

15. Near Bretton Woods, New Hampshire
16. View from Mount Hogback, Vermont
17. Lebanon, Connecticut
18. View from Gillette Castle, Connecticut
19. Hotel Mount Washington, Bretton Woods, New Hampshire
20, 21. Near Stafford Springs, Connecticut
22. Harvest near Storrs, Connecticut
23. Near Essex, Massachusetts
24. Near Cutler, Maine
25. Portsmouth, New Hampshire
26. Near Redding, Connecticut
27. Nineteenth-century schoolhouse, Shelburne Museum, Vermont
28, 29. Henrique's Barber Shop, Eastport, Maine
30. Chrysler car, near Springfield, Massachusetts
31. Ruthella's Beauty Shop, Eastport, Maine
32, 33. Farm near Keene, New Hampshire
34. Presidential View Cabins, Twin Mountain, New Hampshire
35. Scrub near Hancock, New Hampshire
36. Cadillac car, Deep River, Connecticut
37. Scrub near Hancock, New Hampshire
38. Athol, Massachusetts
39. Near Concord, Massachusetts

40. Near Gilmanton, New Hampshire
41. Biddeford, Maine
42. Wentworth, New Hampshire
43. Long Beach, Massachusetts
44. Lake Winnipesaukee, Melvin Village, New Hampshire
45. In the State of Connecticut
46, 47. Rockport, Massachusetts
48, 49. Gloucester, Massachusetts
50. Berlin, New Hampshire
51. Athol, Massachusetts
52. Abandoned factory, Winchendon, Massachusetts
53. Concord, New Hampshire
54. Near South Peacham, Vermont
55. Near Barnet Center, Vermont
56. Papermill in Berlin, New Hampshire
57. Near Rye North Beach, New Hampshire
58. Factory in Orange, Massachusetts
59. Near Rye North Beach, New Hampshire
60, 61. Vanishing Light, near Goshen, Connecticut
62. Near Eaton, Maine
63. Gas station near Bethel, Connecticut
64. Near Bennington, Vermont

65. Near Lebanon, Connecticut

66. Near Pittsfield, Massachusetts

67. Willimantic, Connecticut

68. Evening sun near Percy, Maine

69. Near Jonesboro, Maine

70. Near Kennebunkport, Maine

71. Gloucester, Massachusetts

72. Near Saint Albans, Vermont

73. Hotel in Burlington, Vermont

74. Inn at Amherst, Massachusetts

75. Presidential Waterbed Hotel, Conway, New Hampshire

76. Saint Albans, Vermont

77. Movie theater in Norwich, Connecticut

78. Gilley's Lunch Cart, Portsmouth, New Hampshire

79. Fishtale Diner, Newburyport, Massachusetts

80. Tommy's Diner, Newport, Rhode Island

The Plates

1

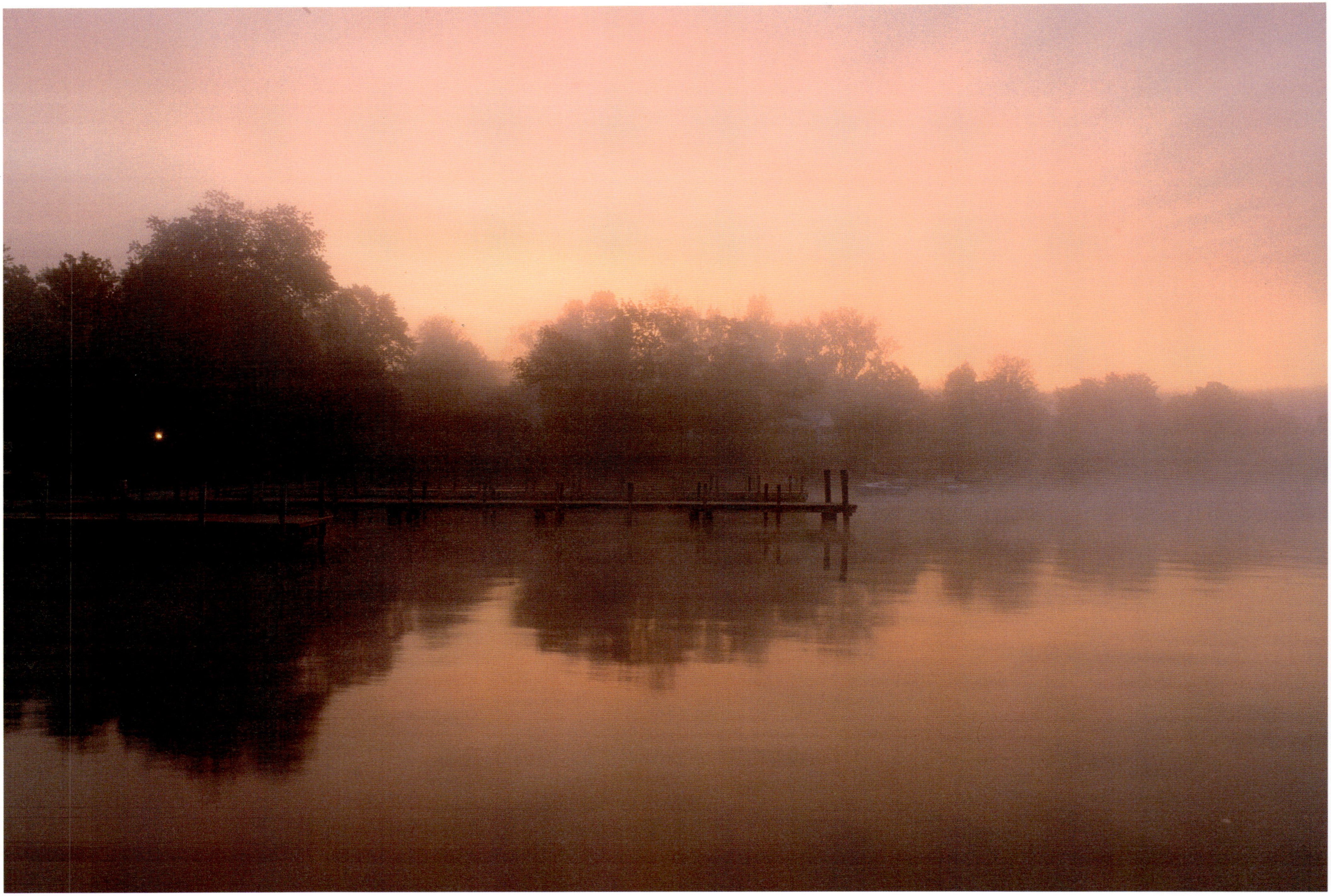

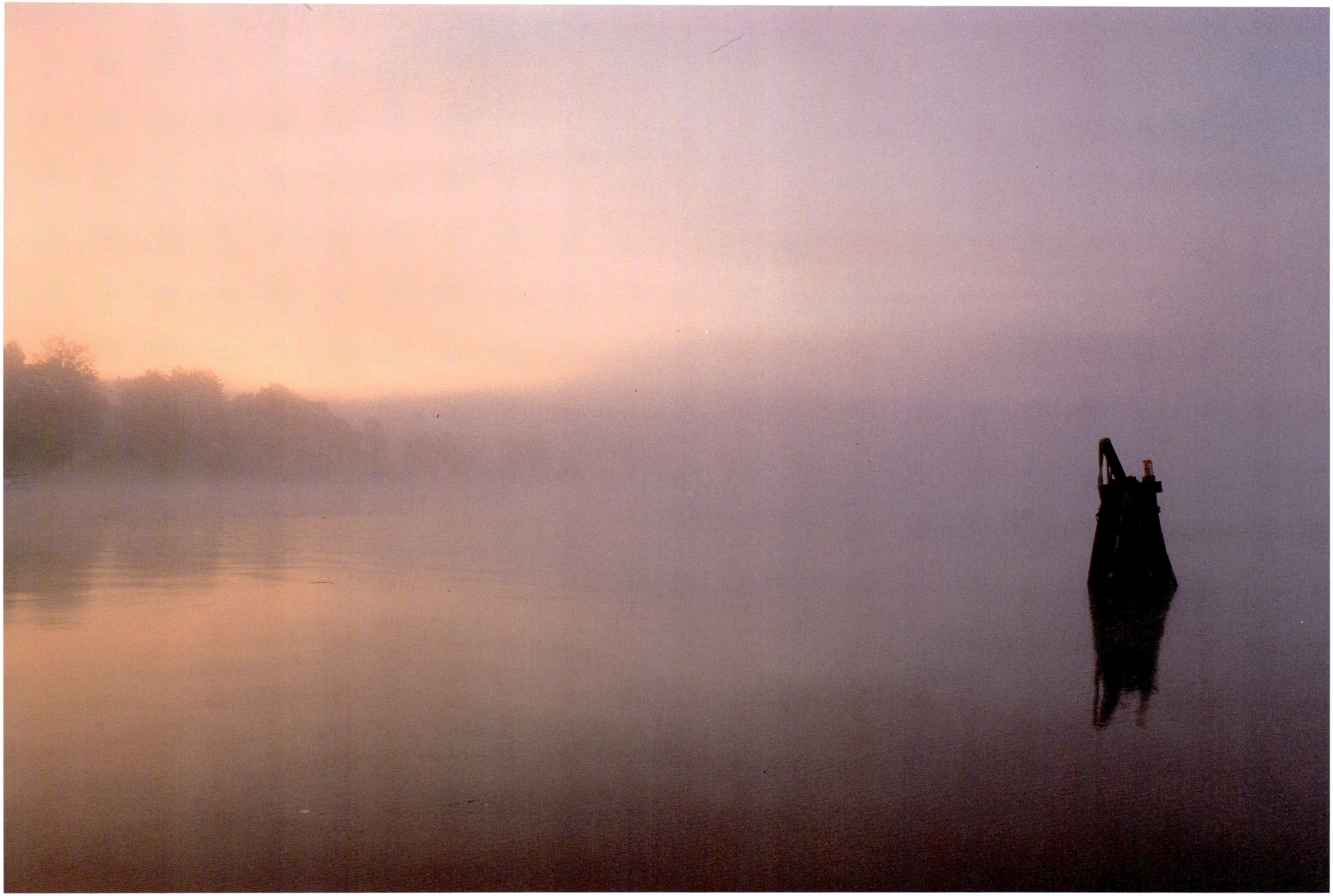

4

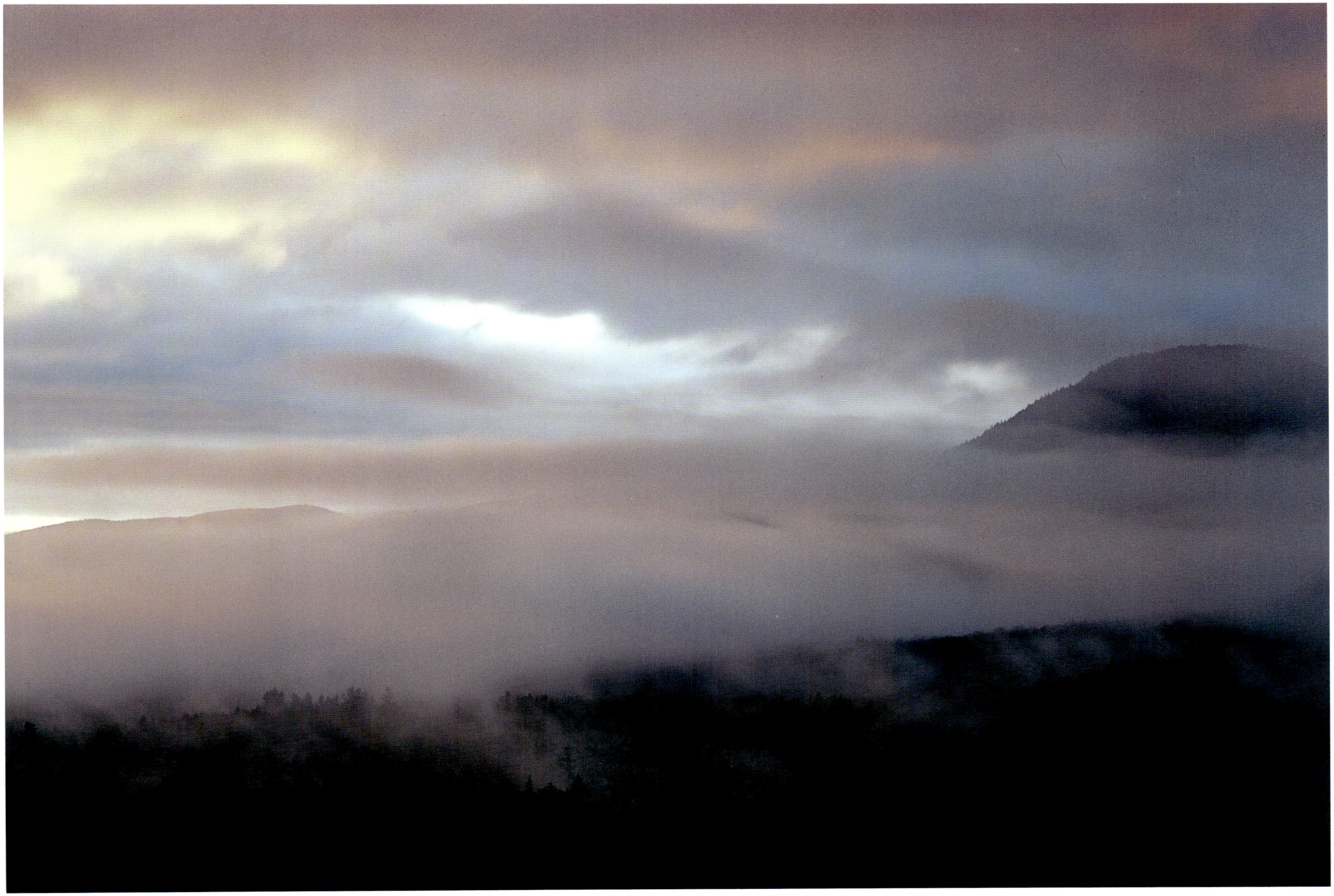

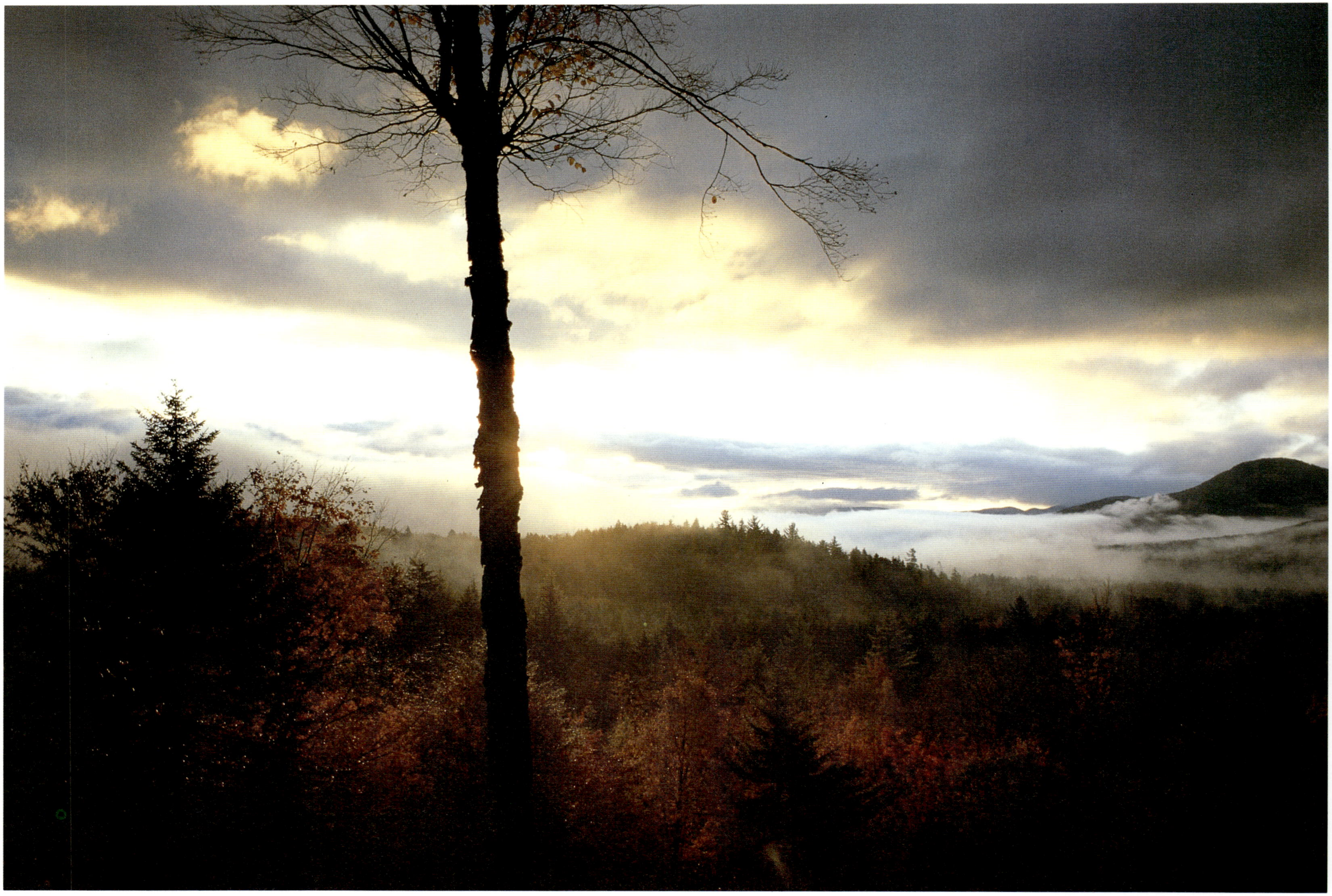

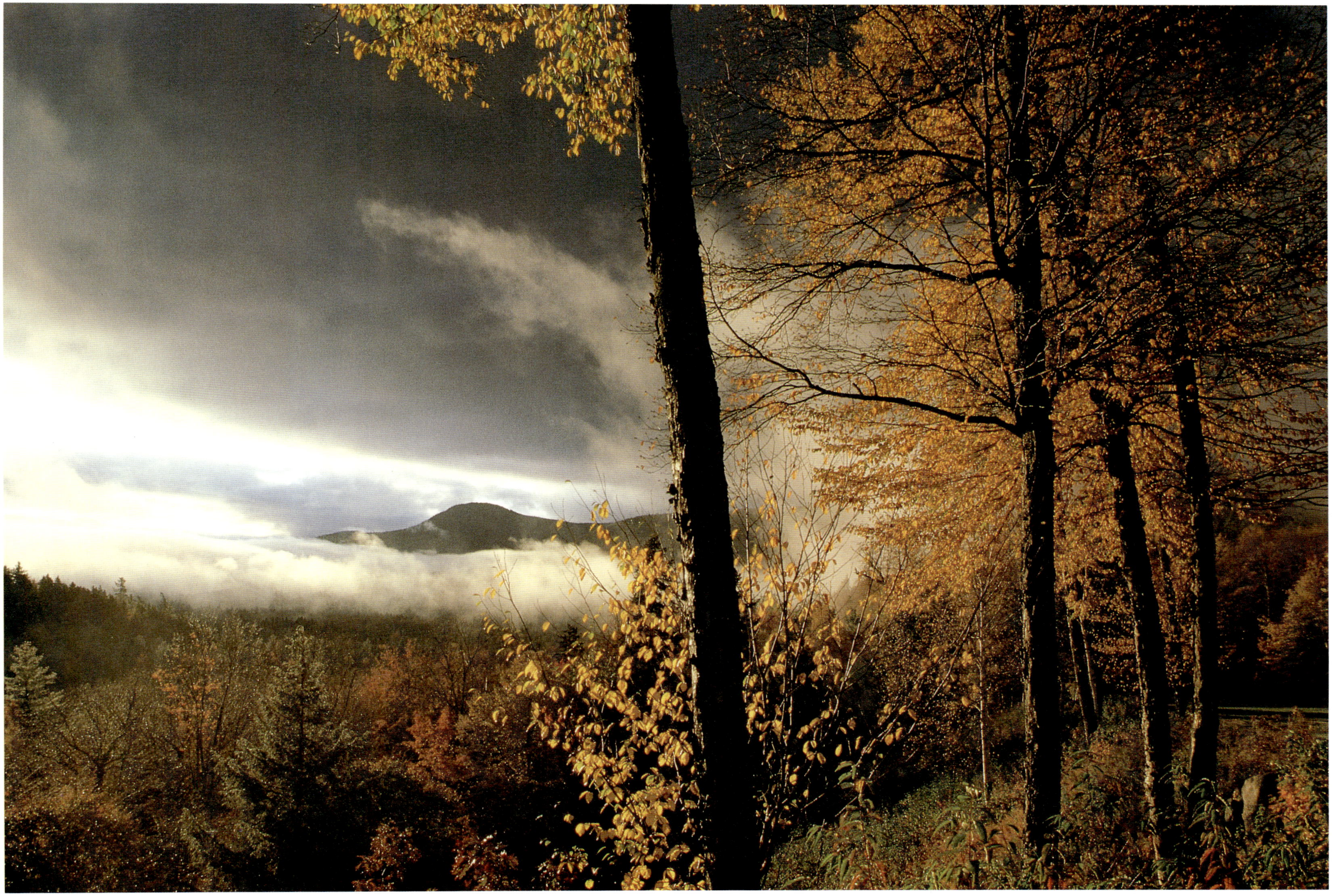

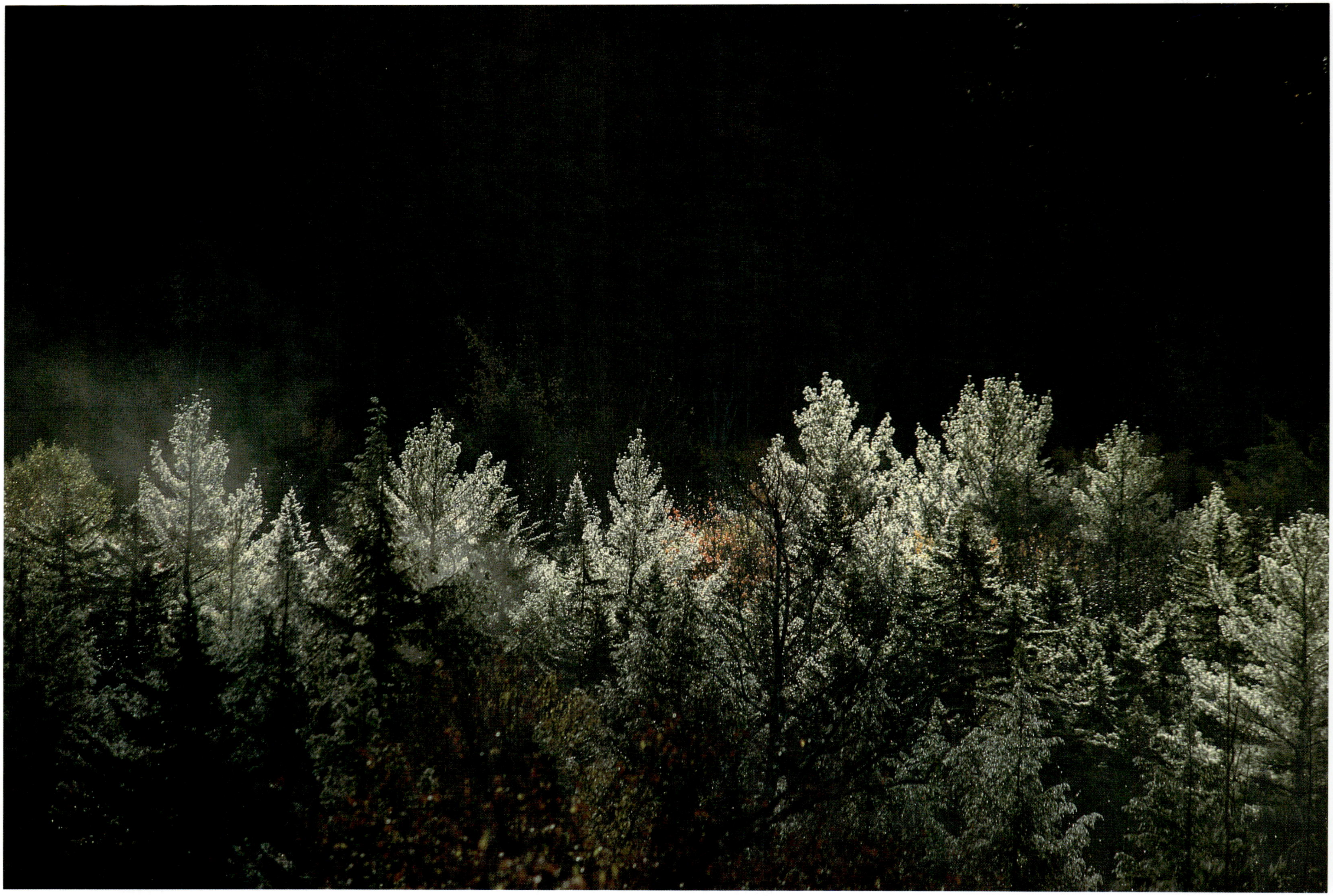

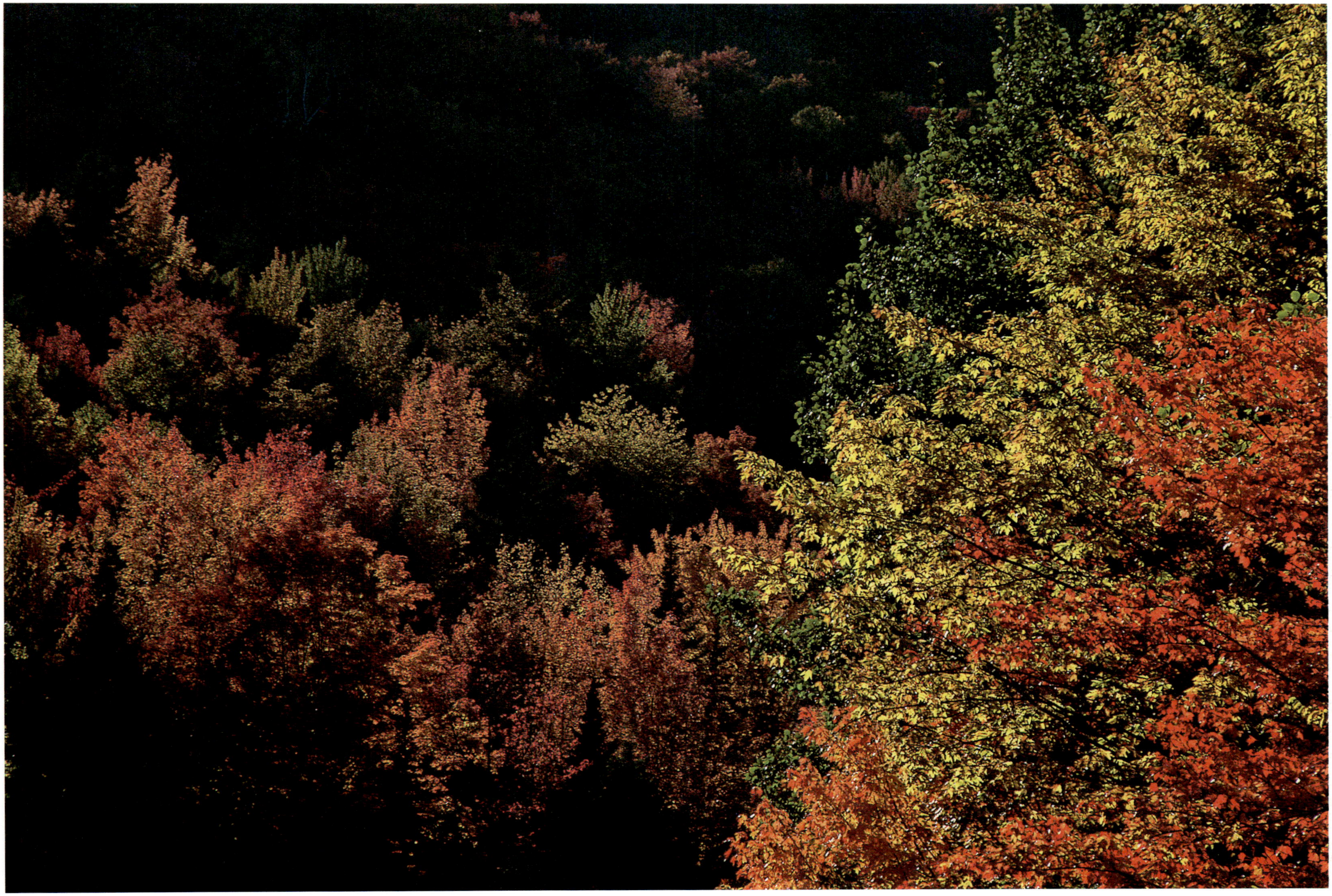

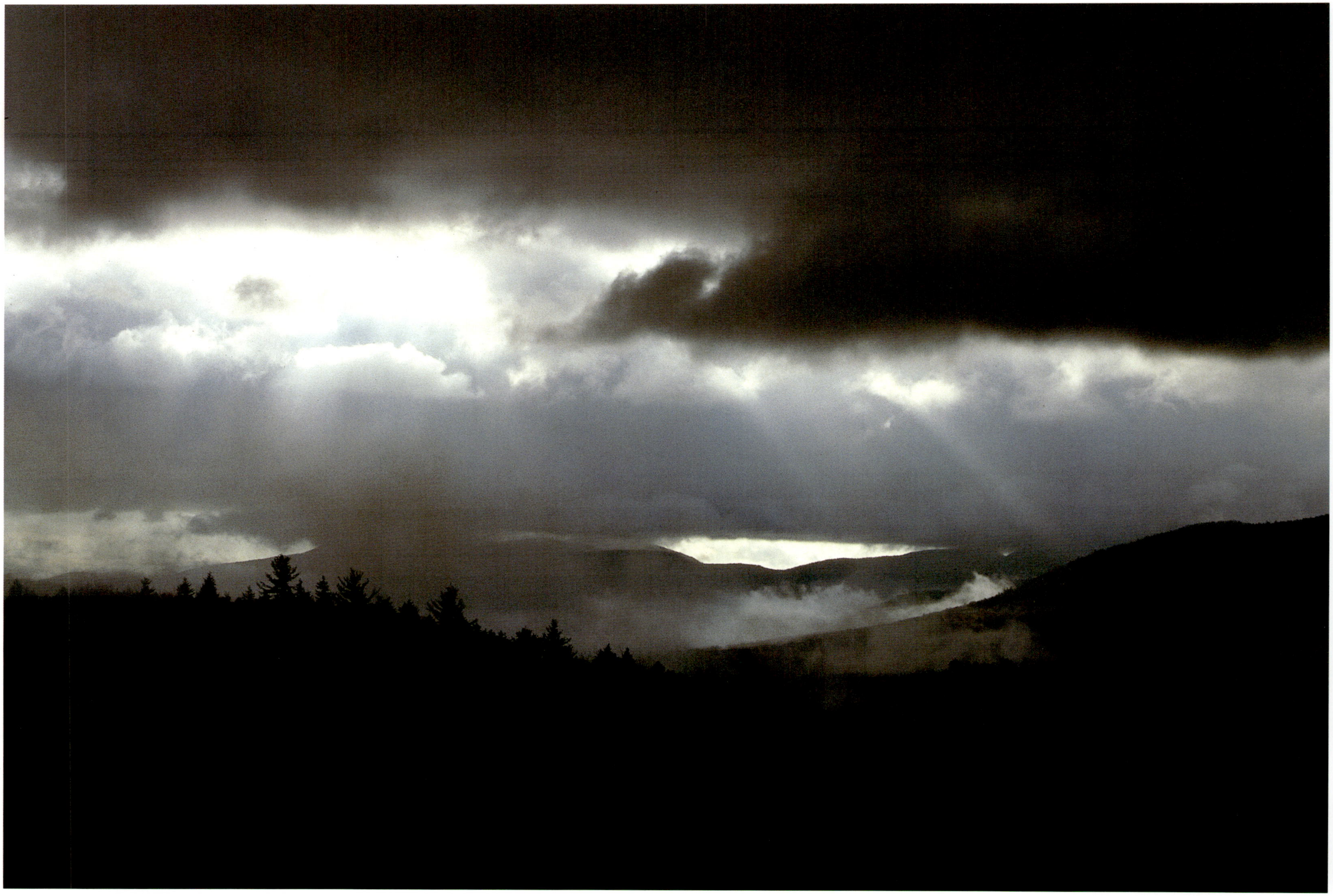

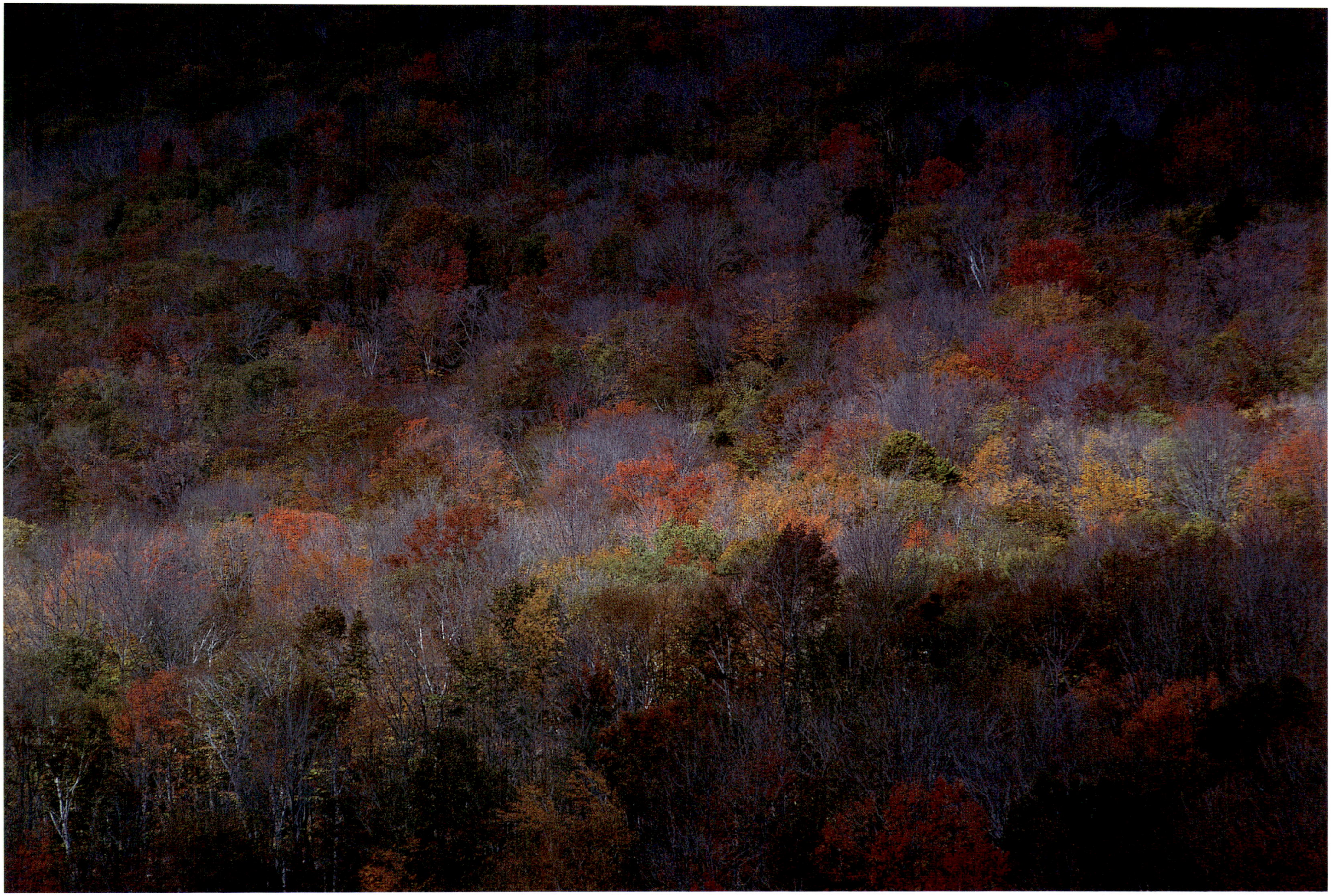

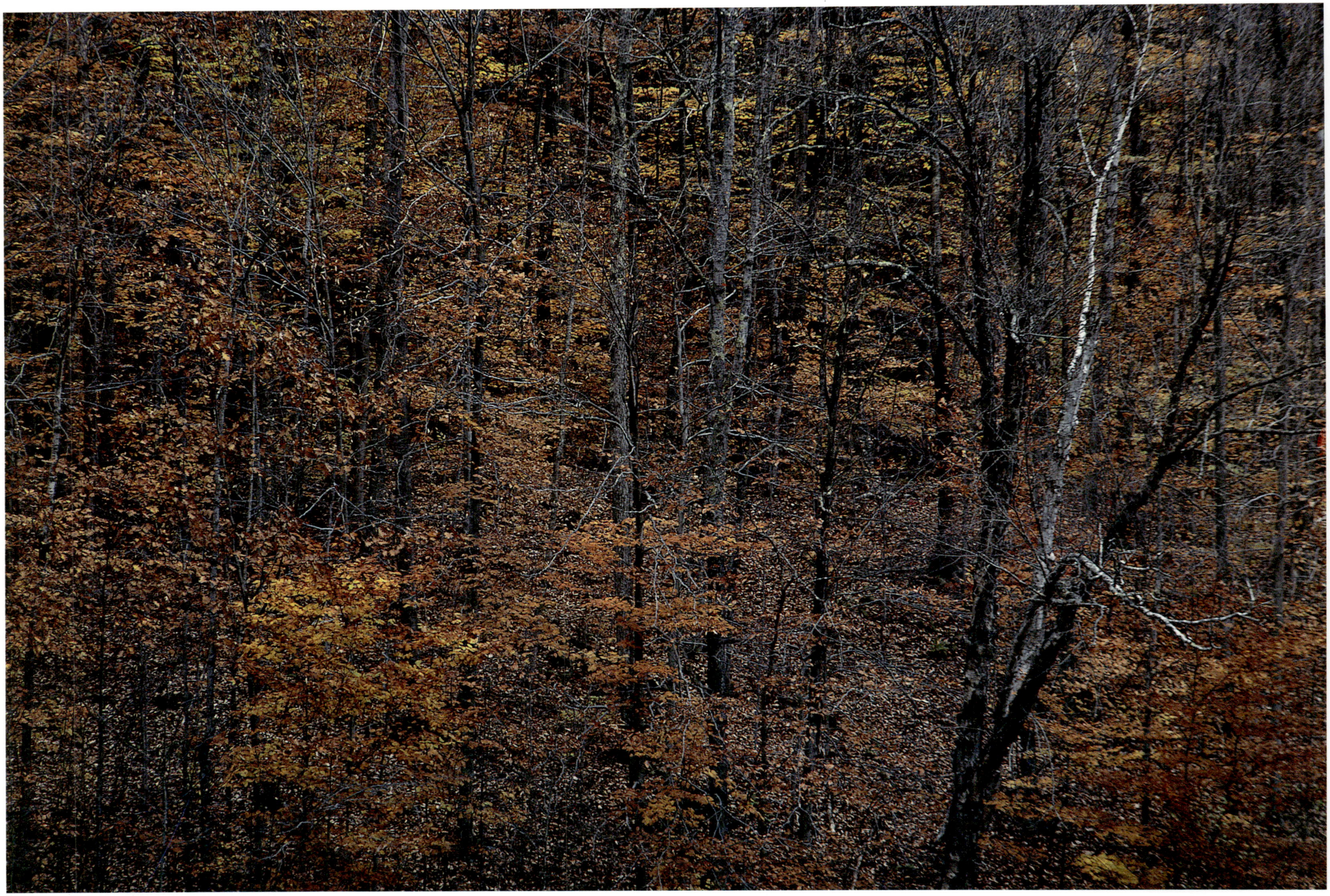

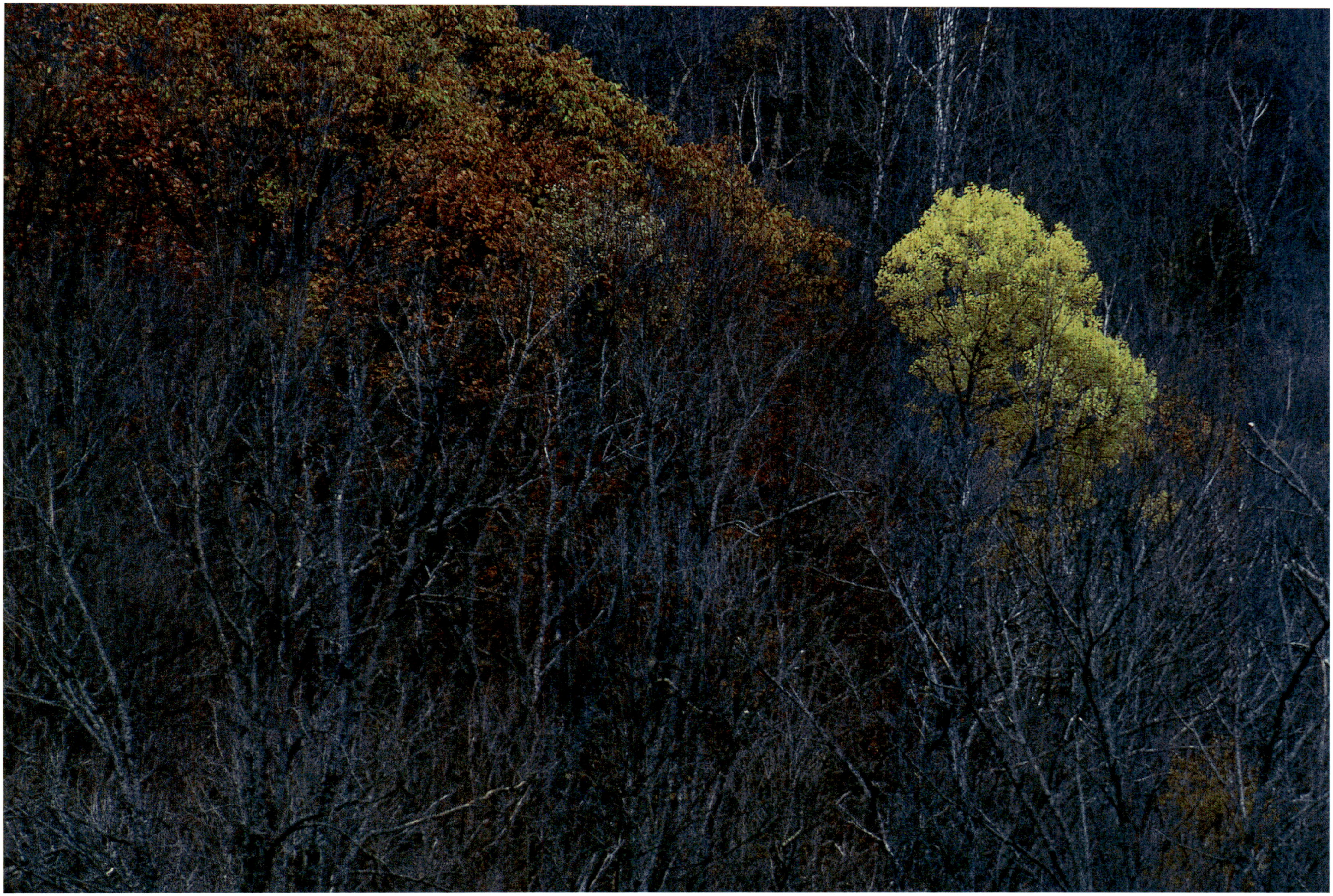

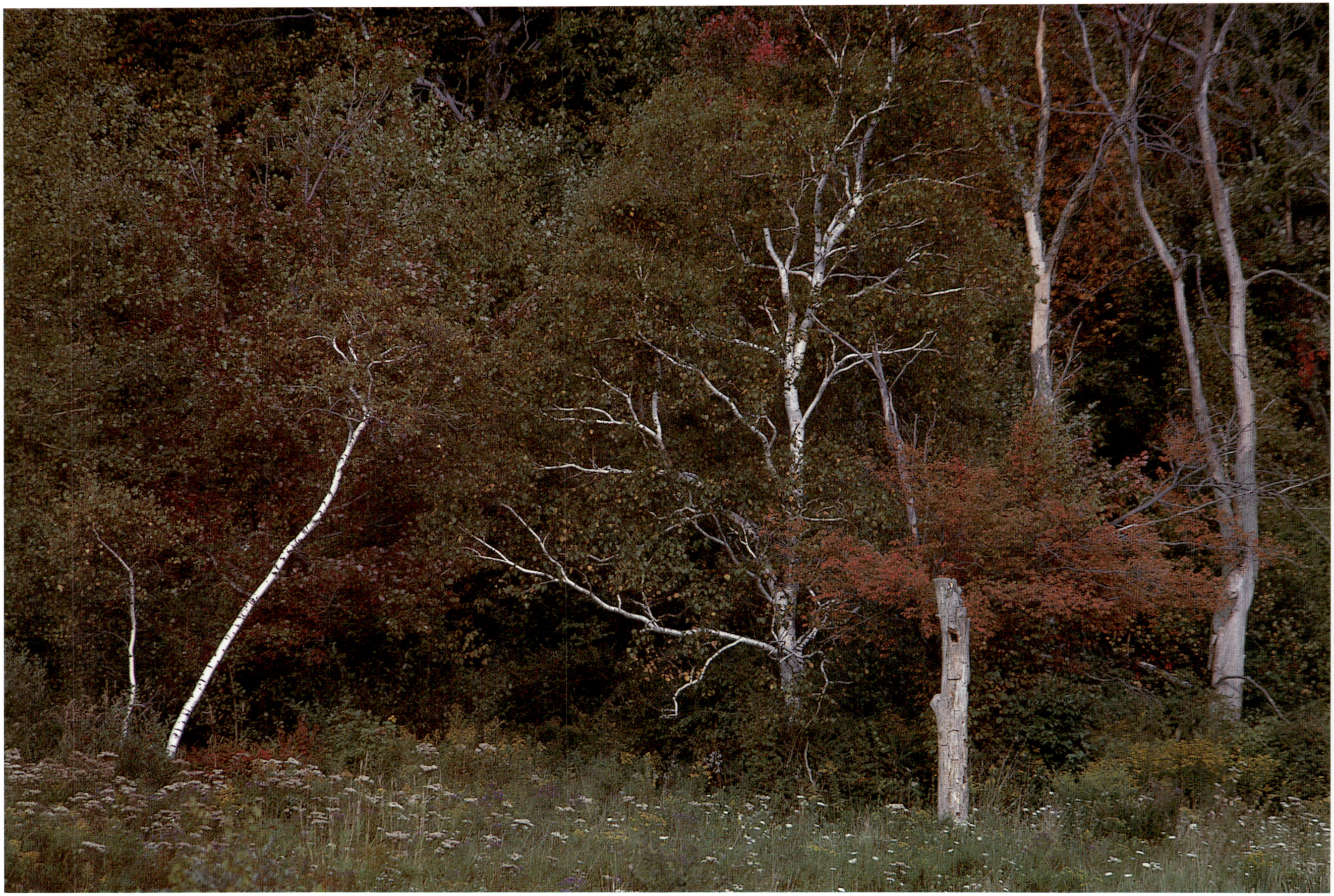

15

16

17

18

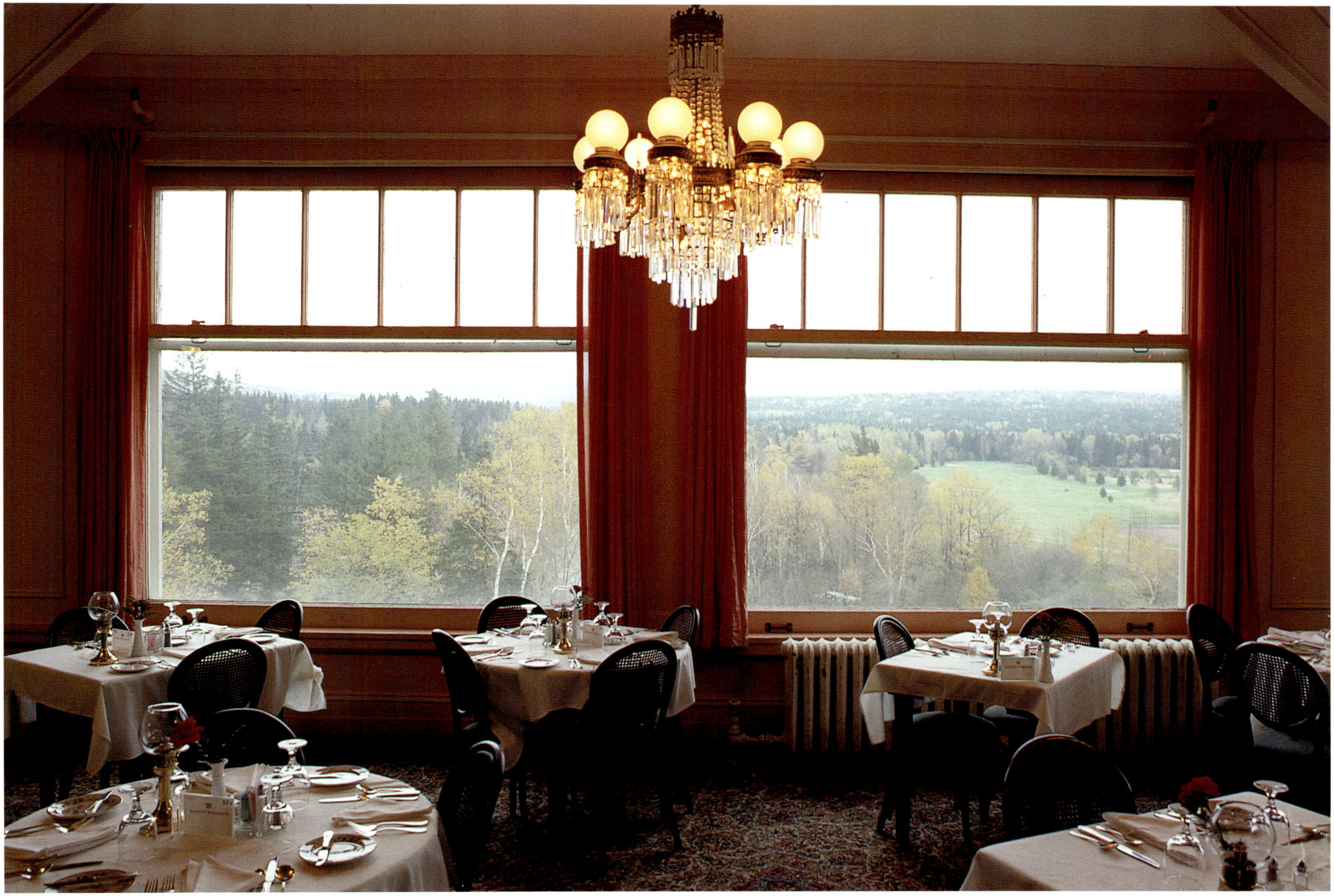

20

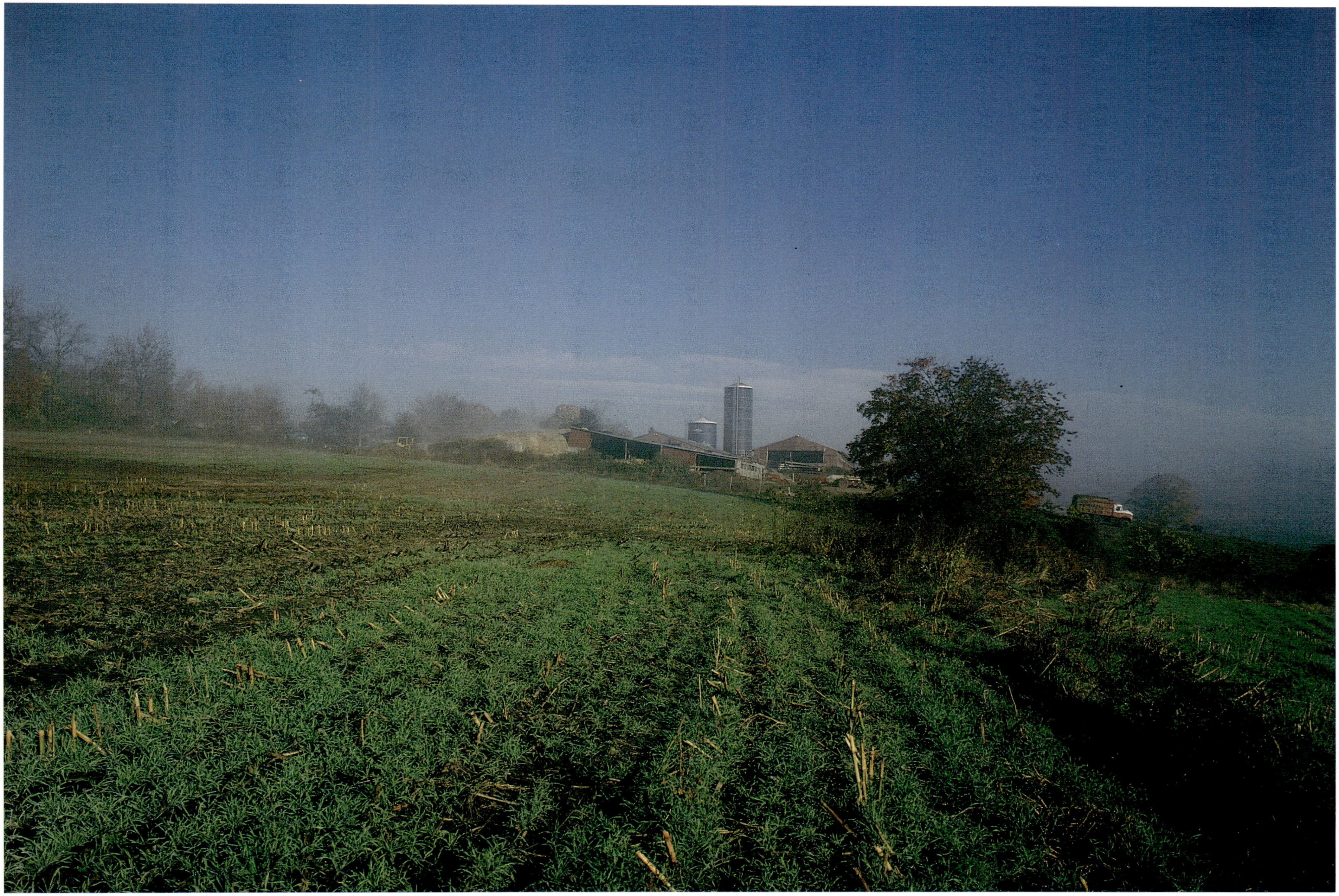

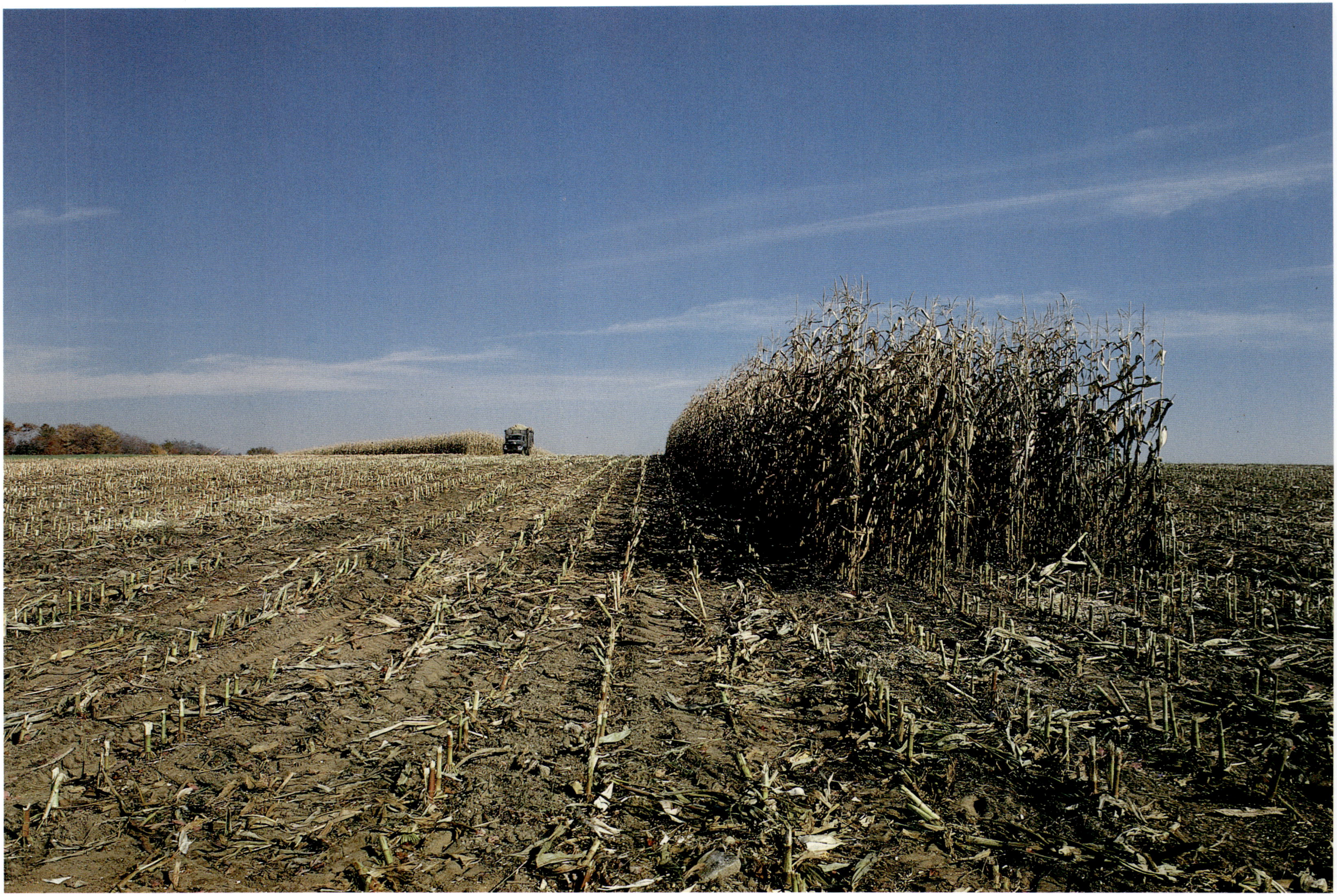

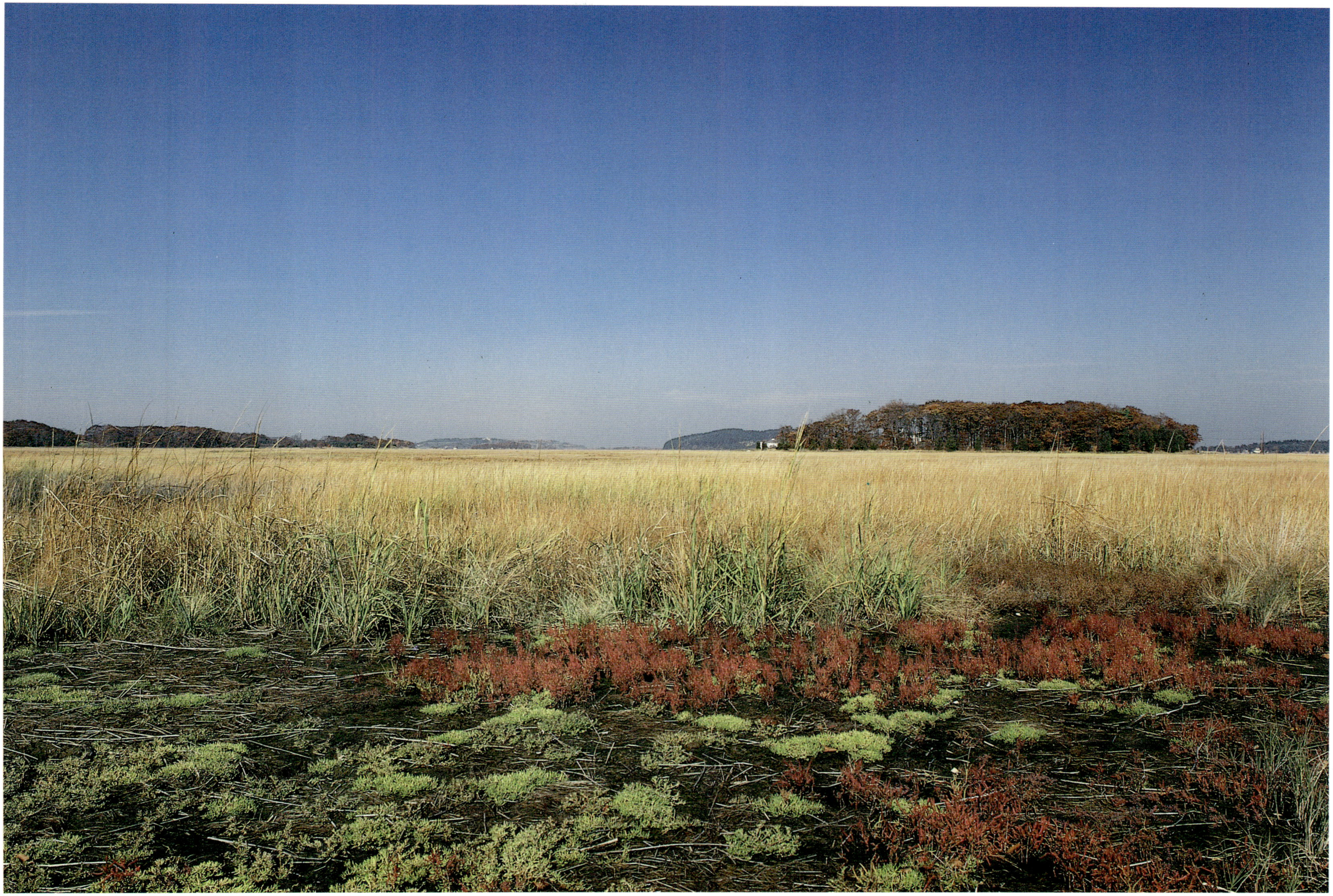

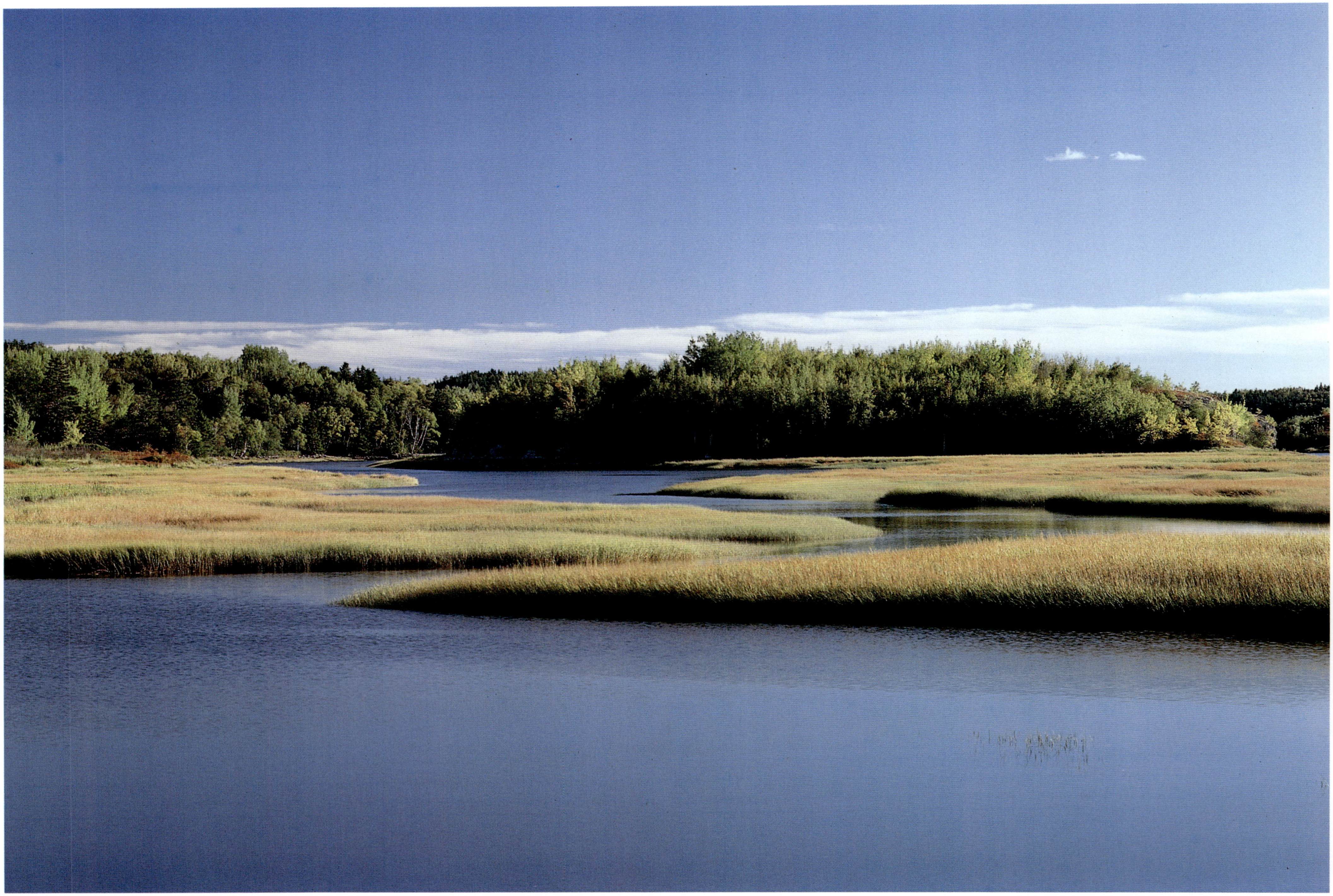

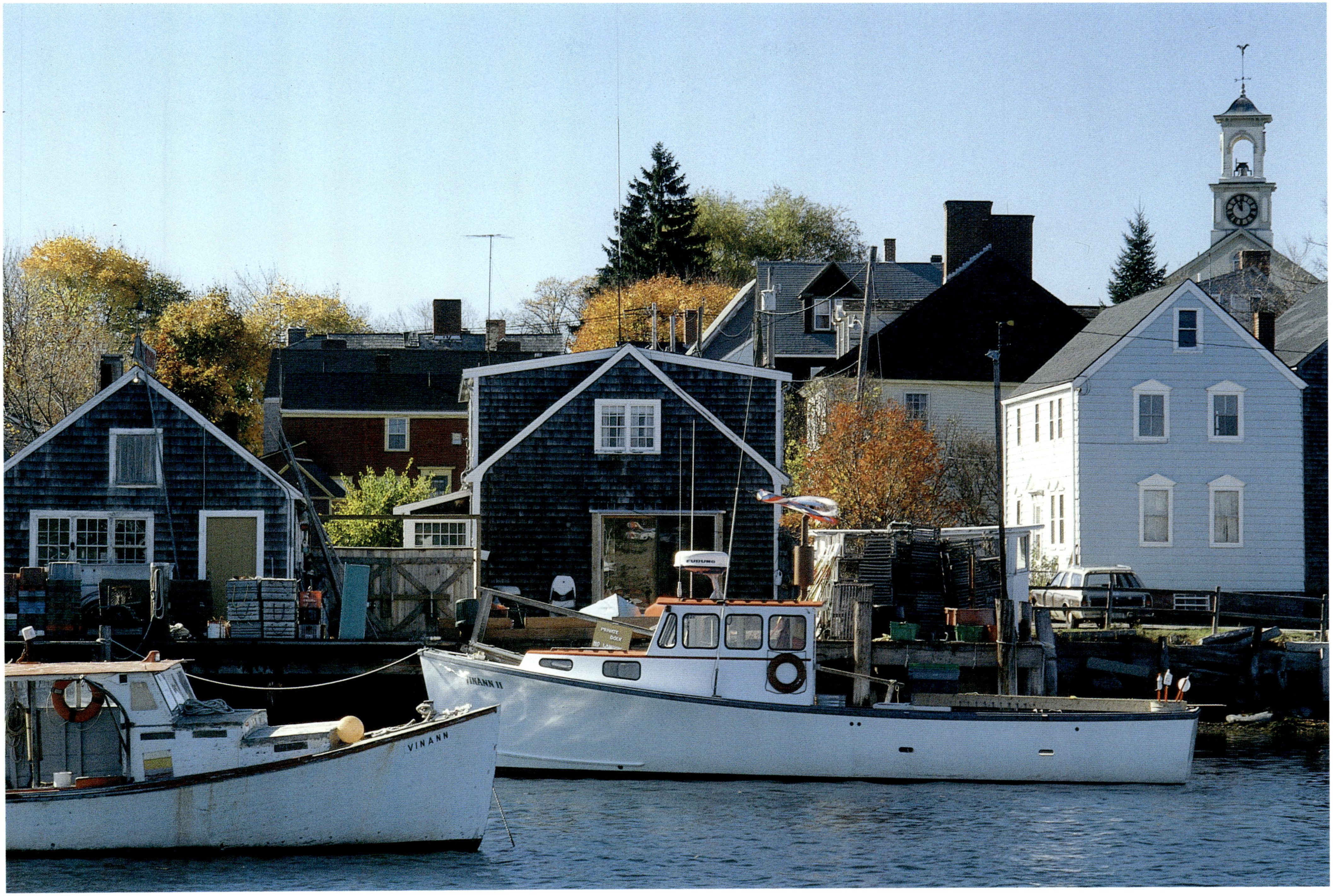
VINANN

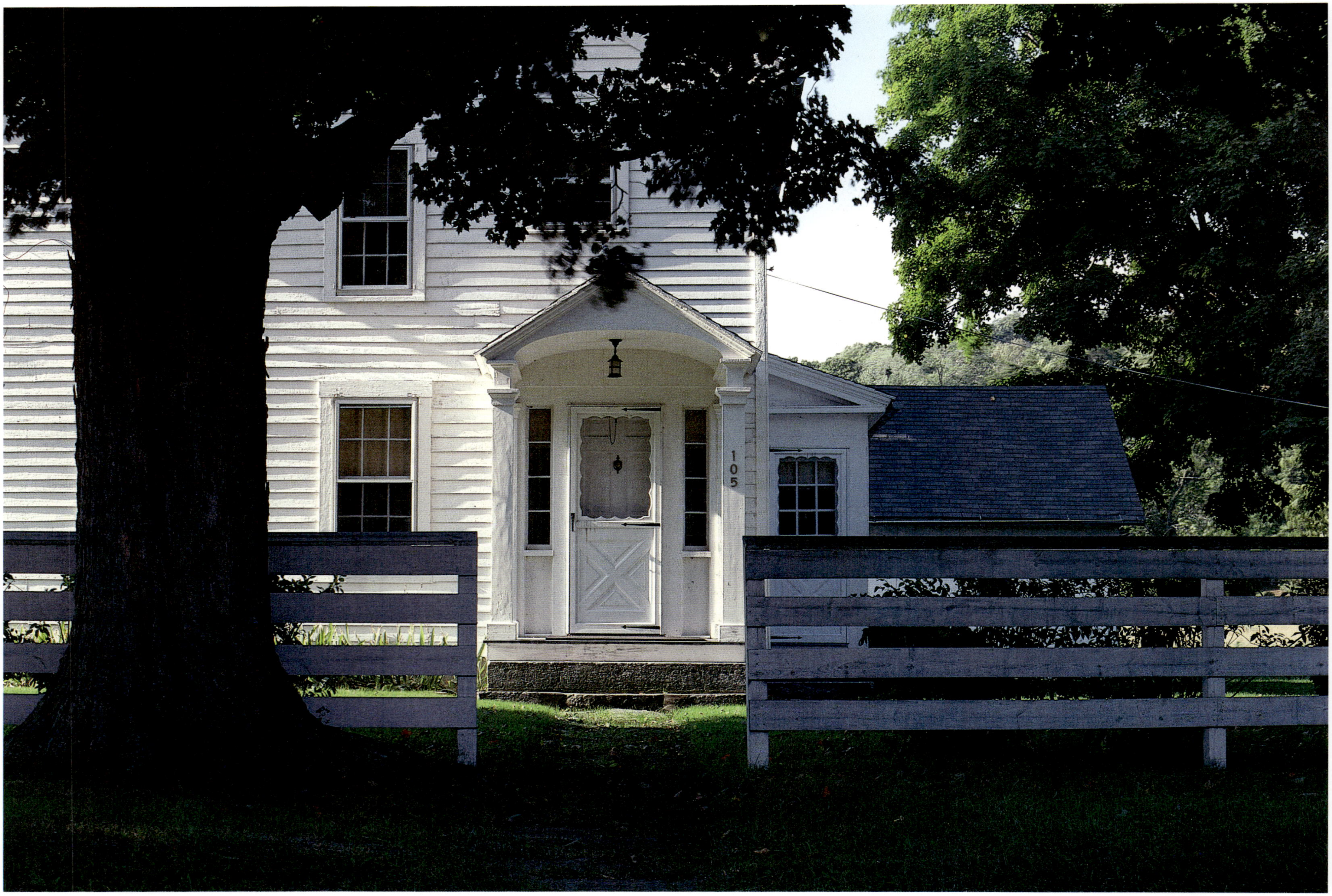
105

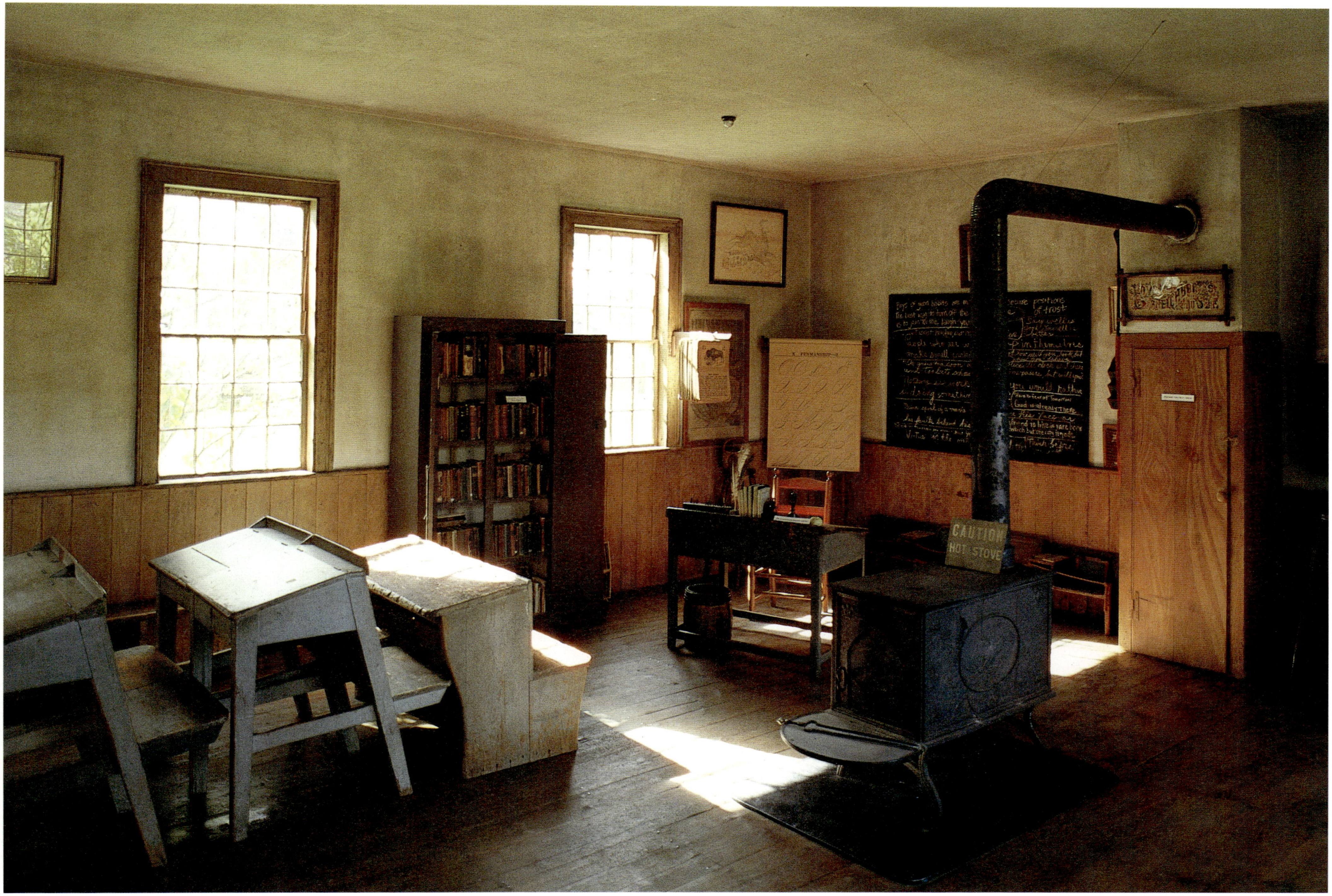
CAUTION
HOT STOVE

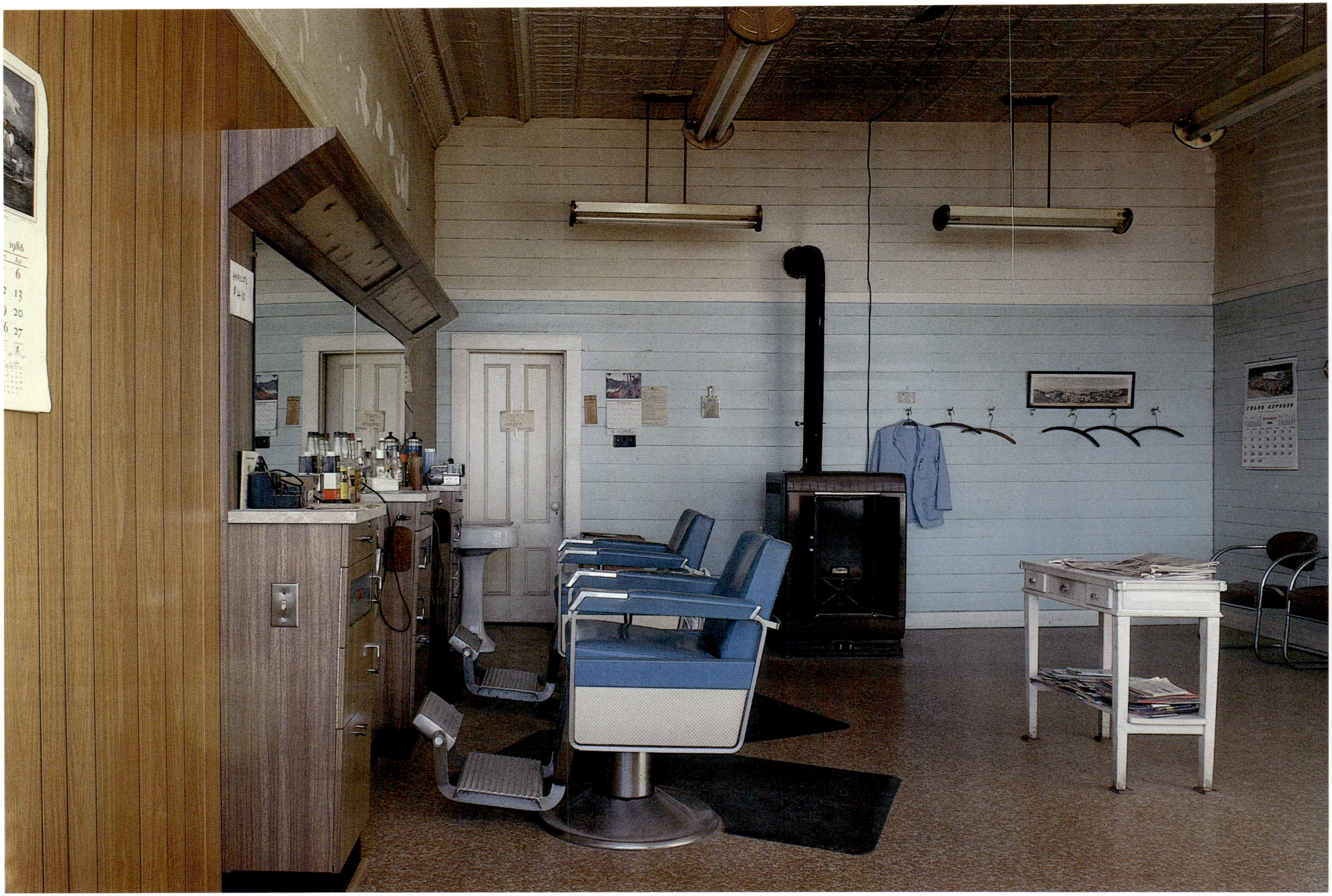

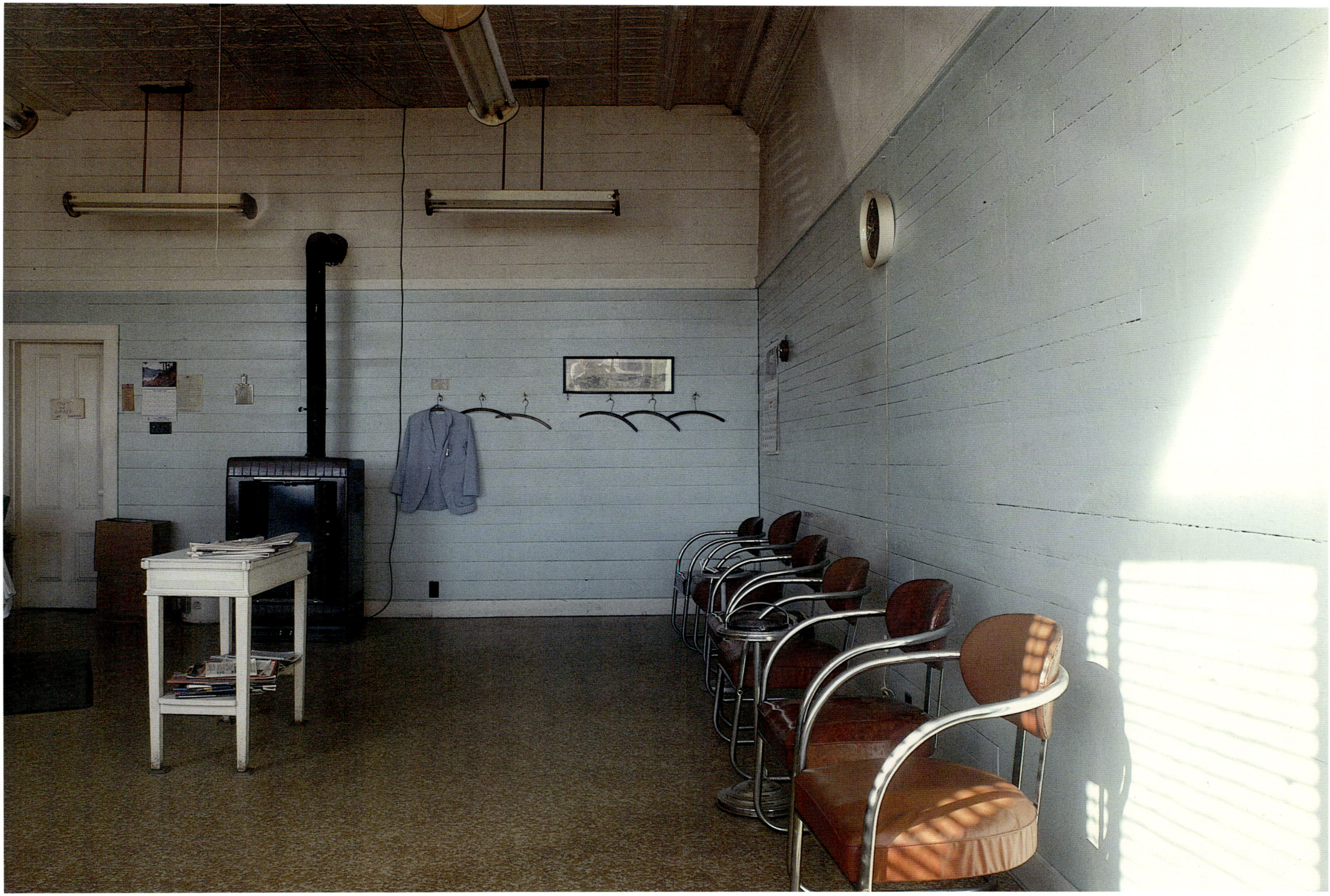

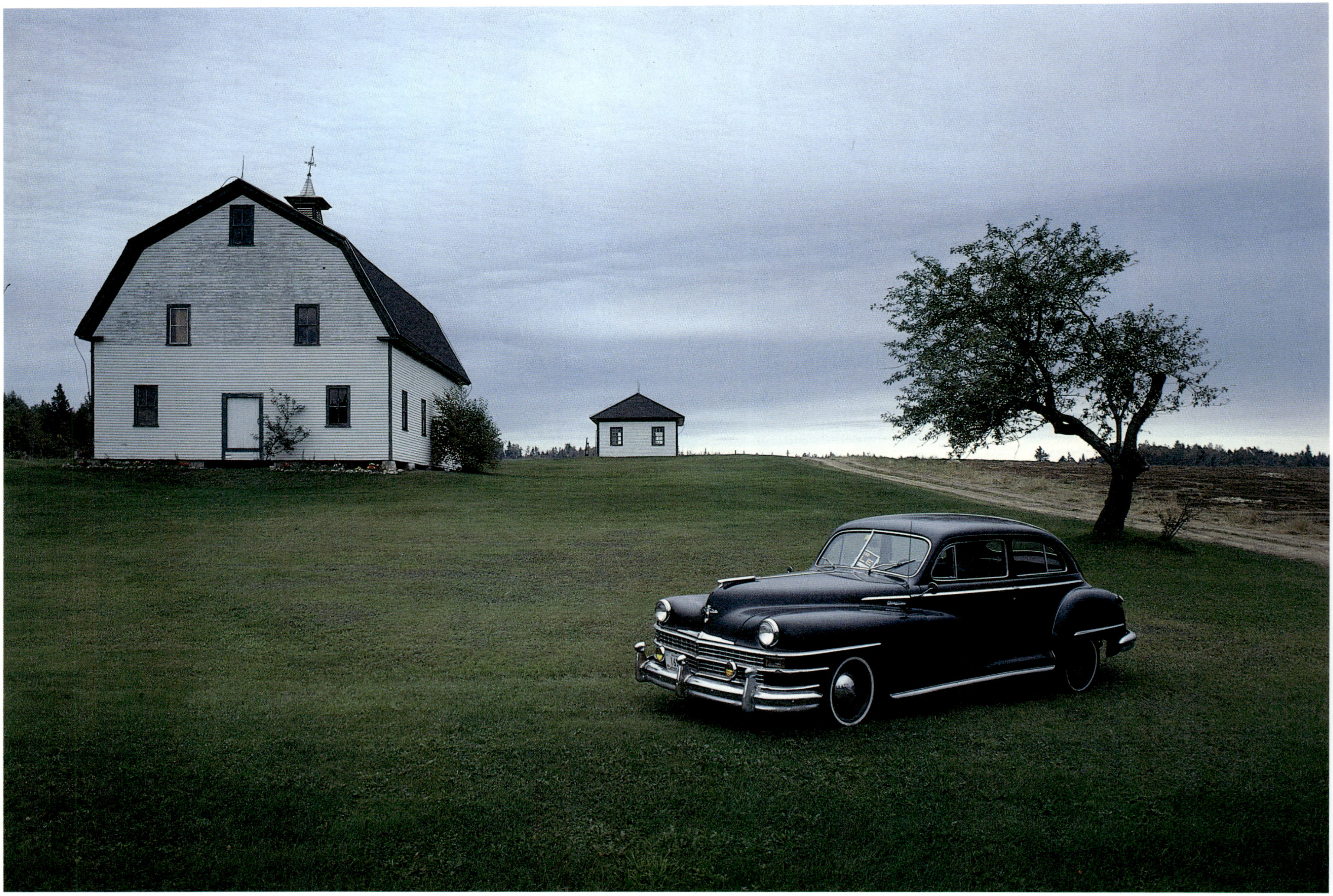

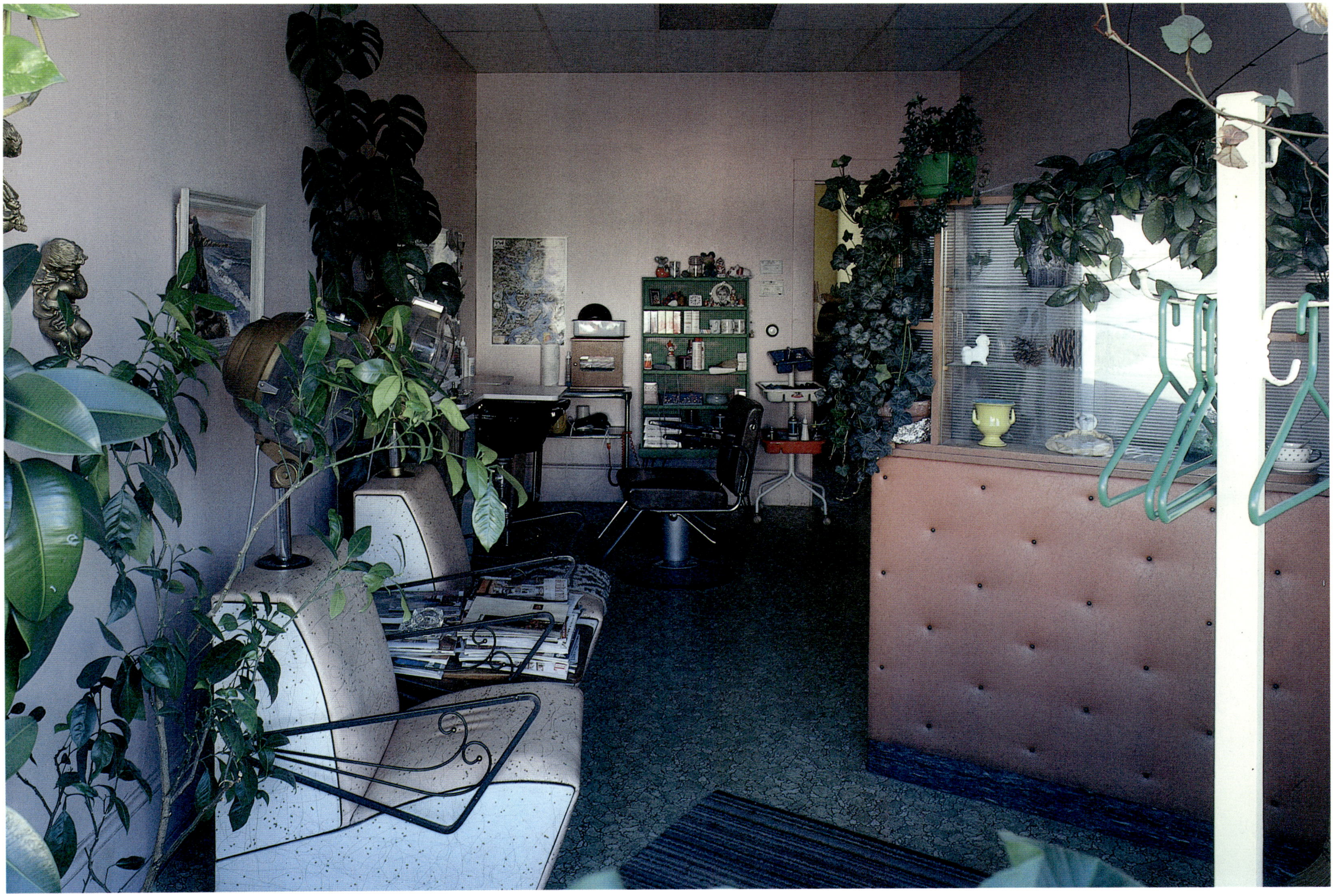

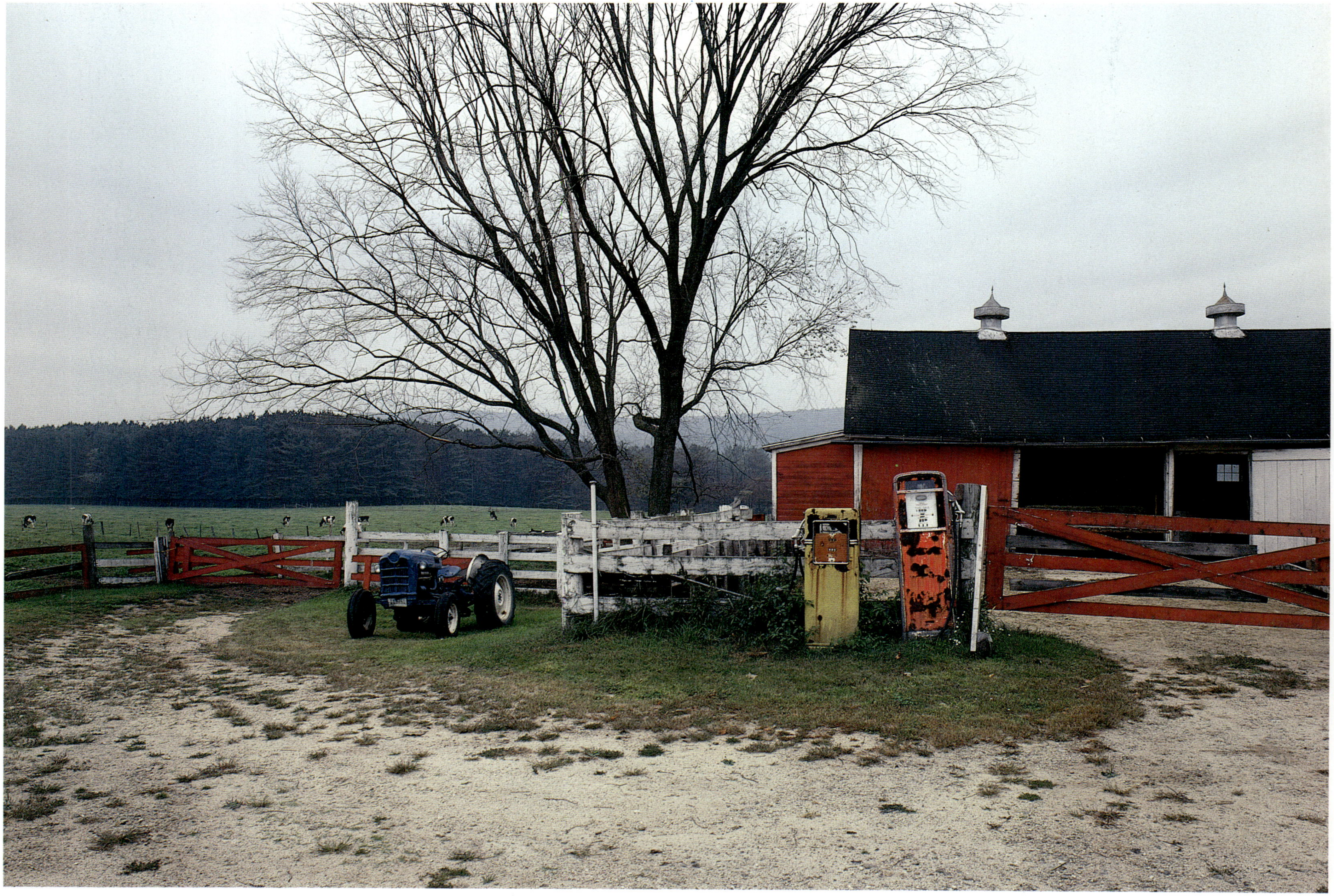

33

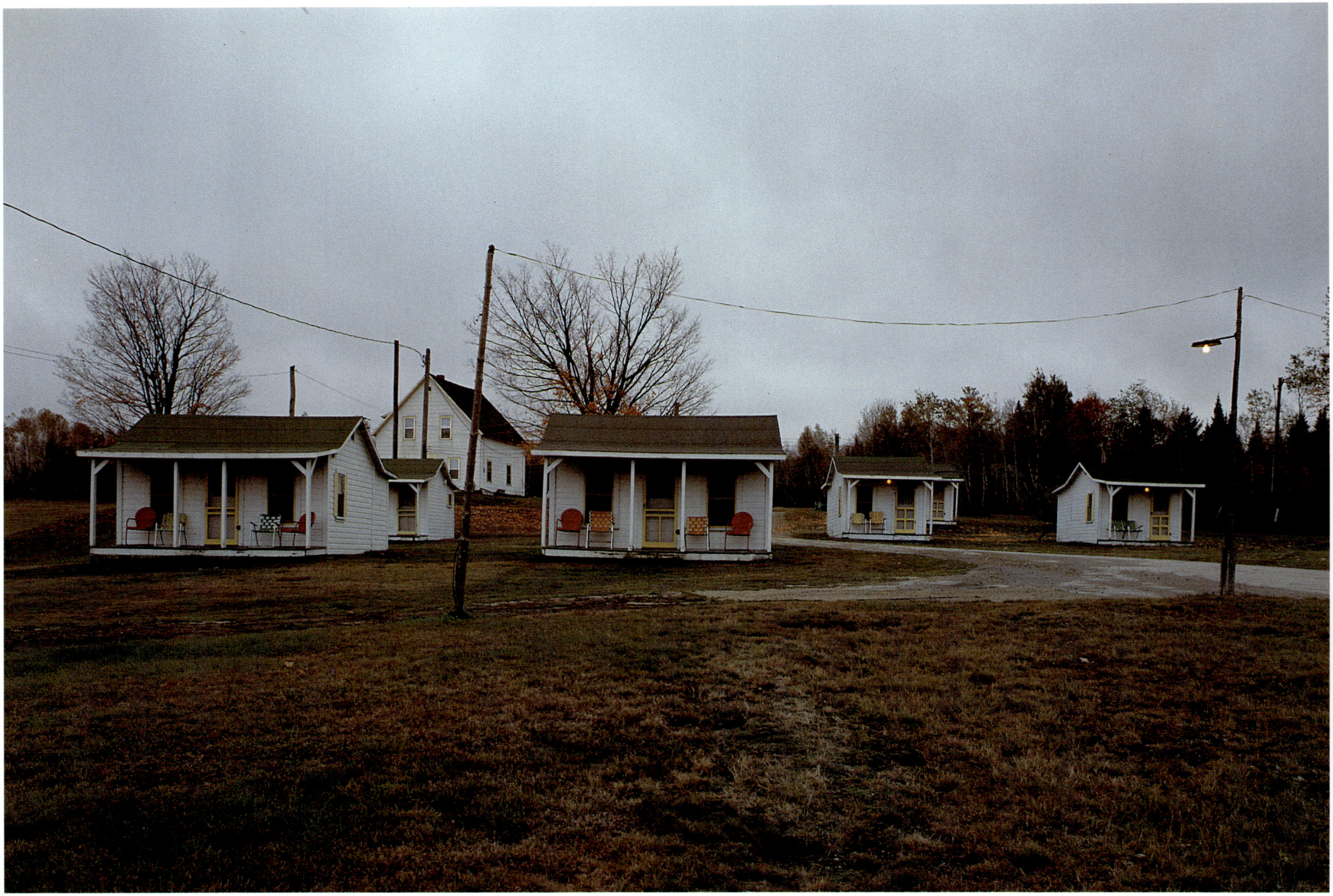

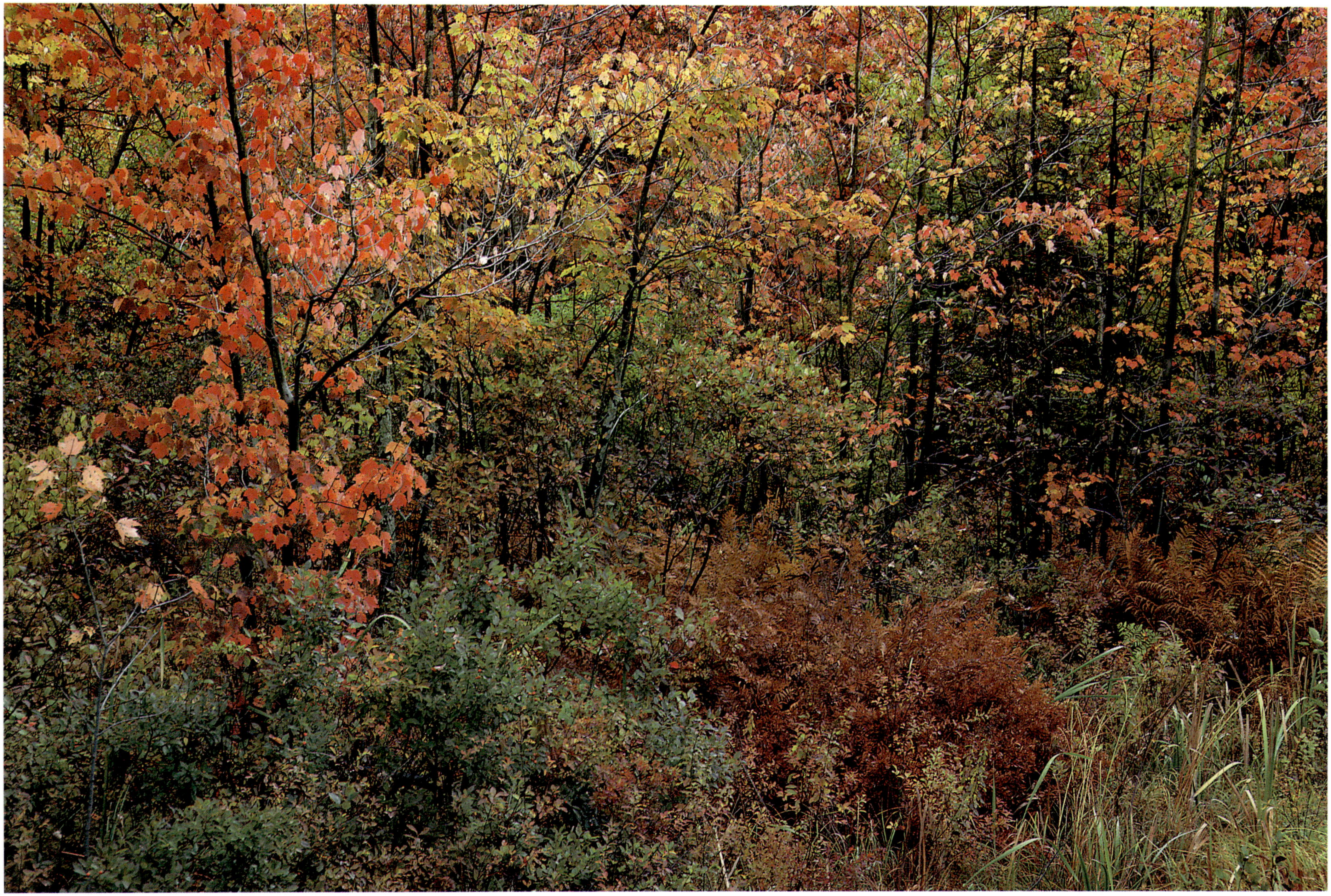

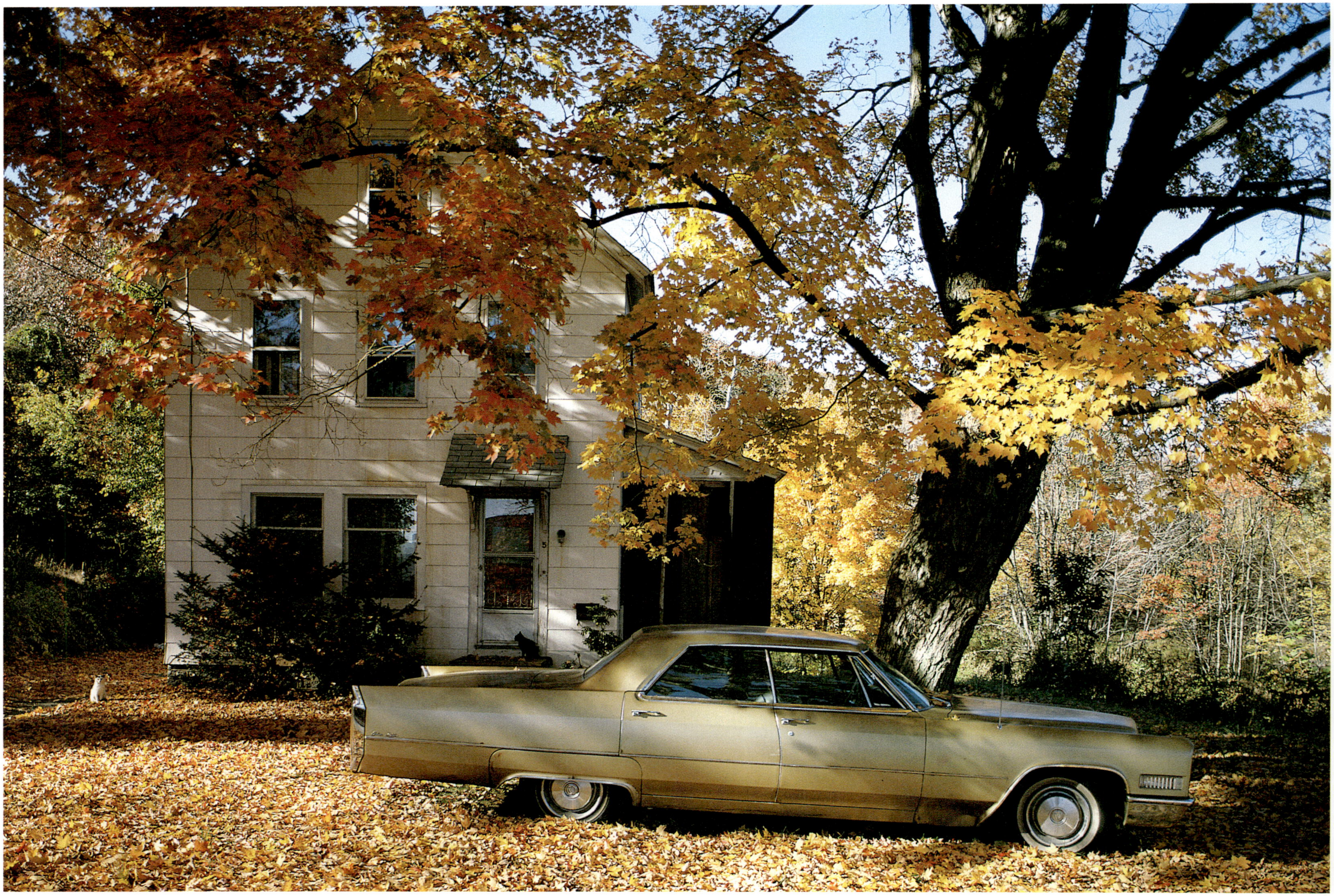

37

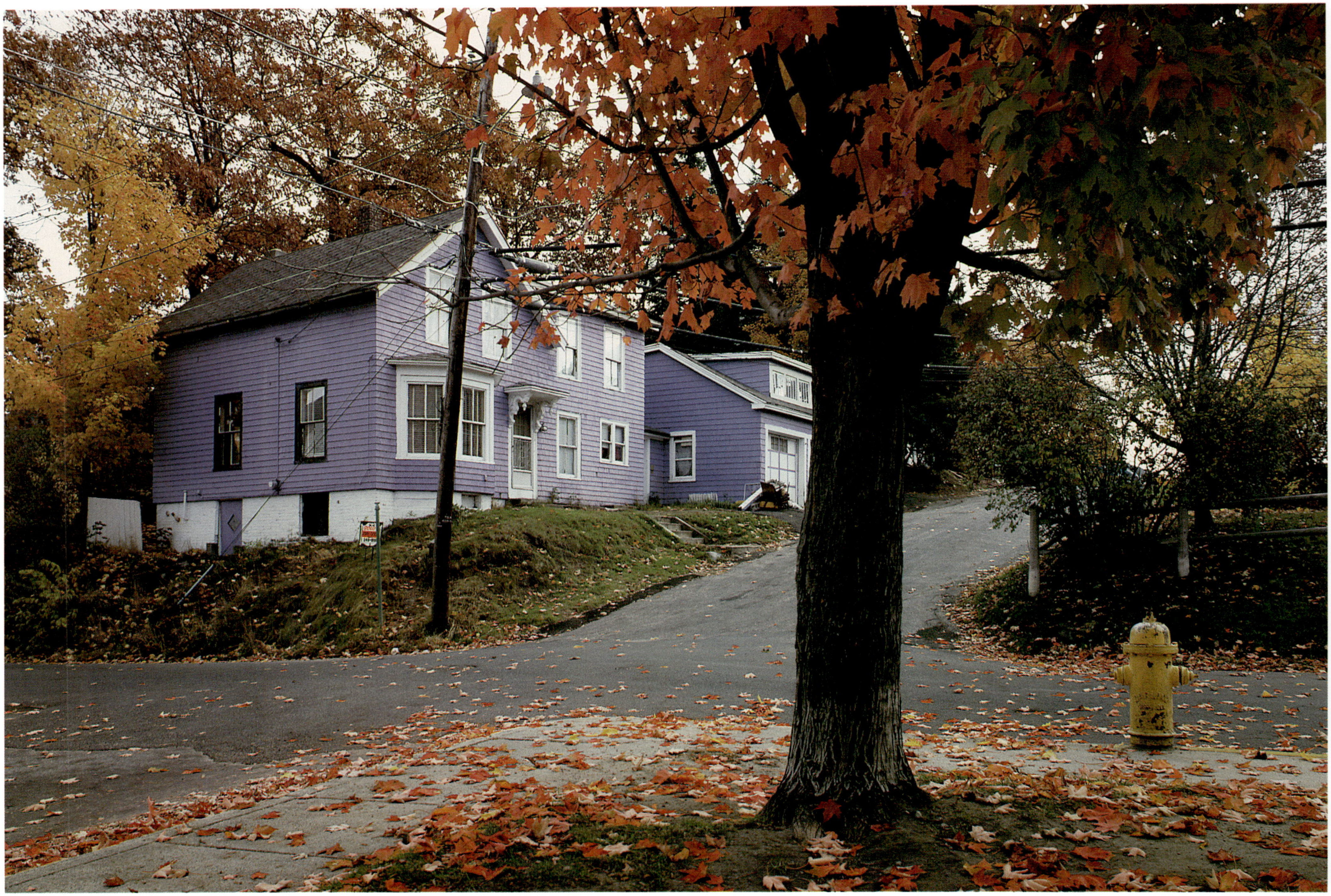

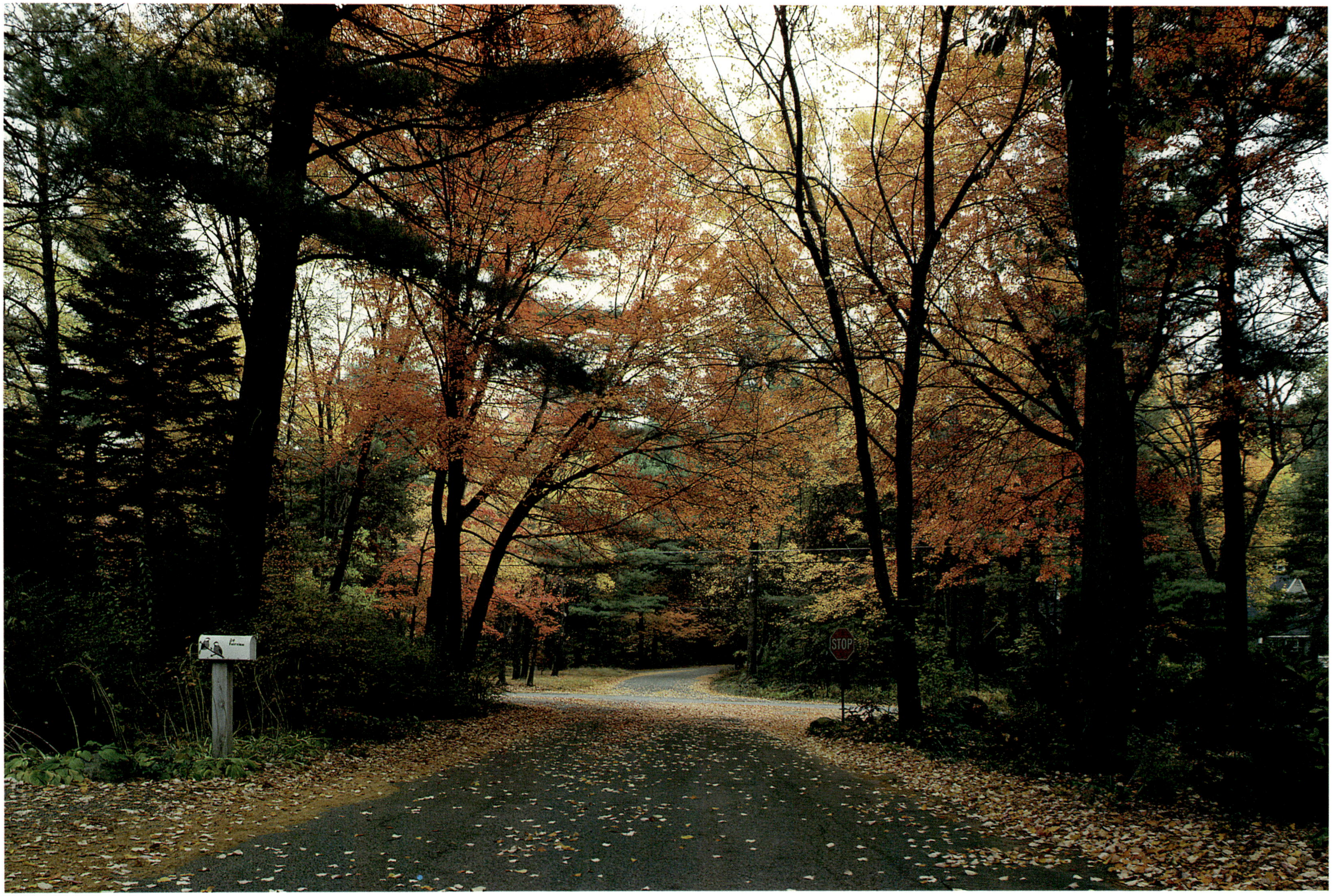
STOP

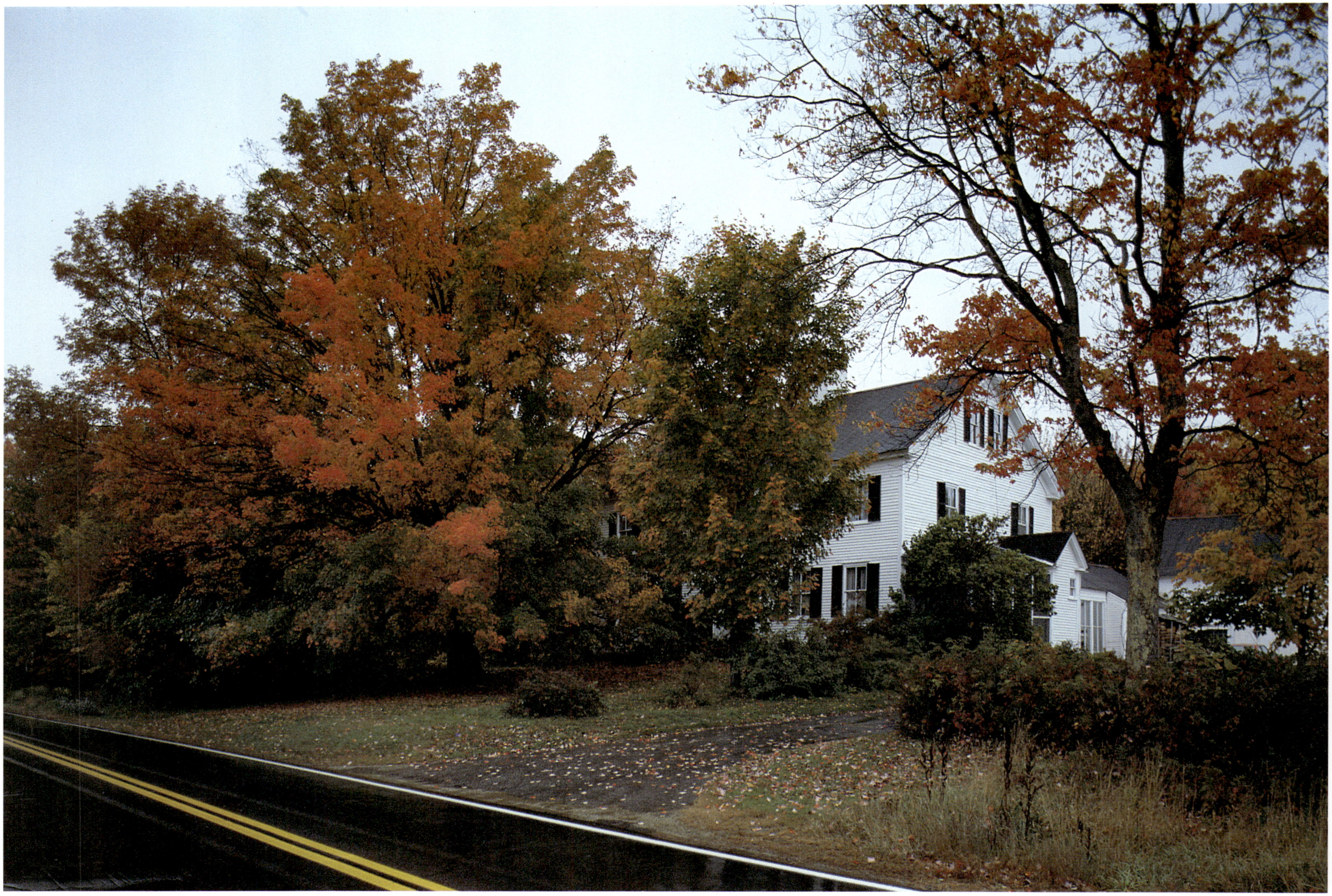

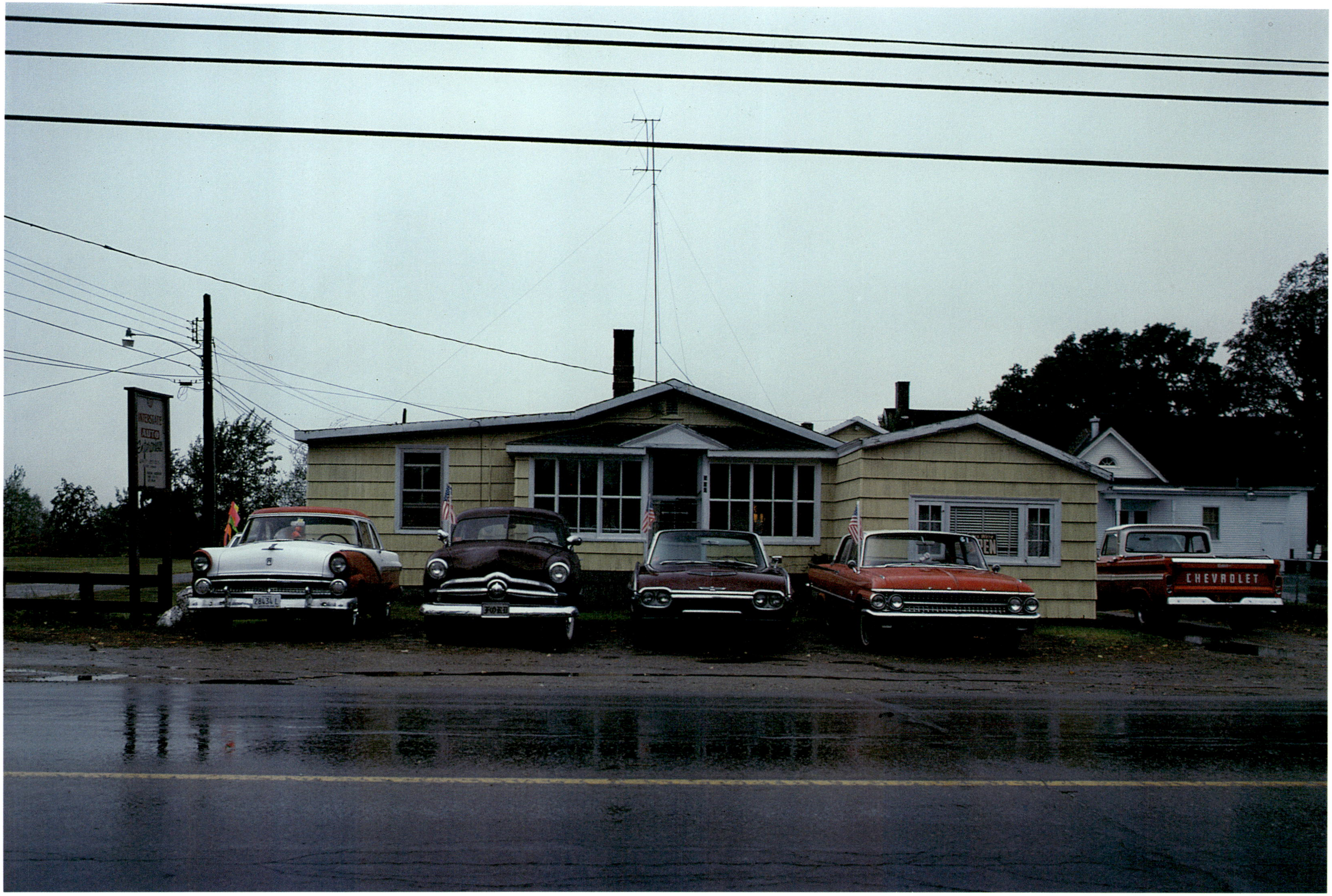
CHEVROLET

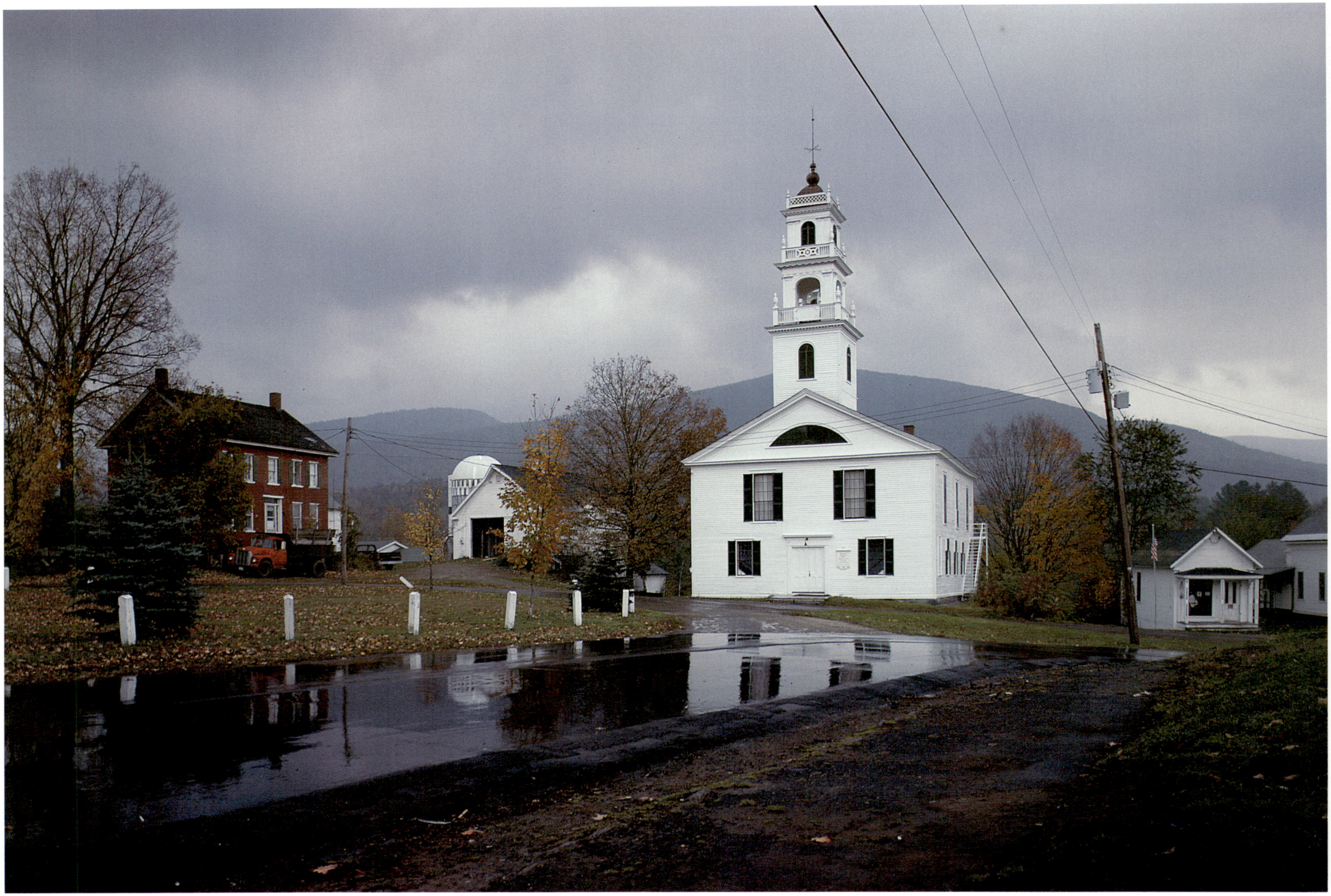

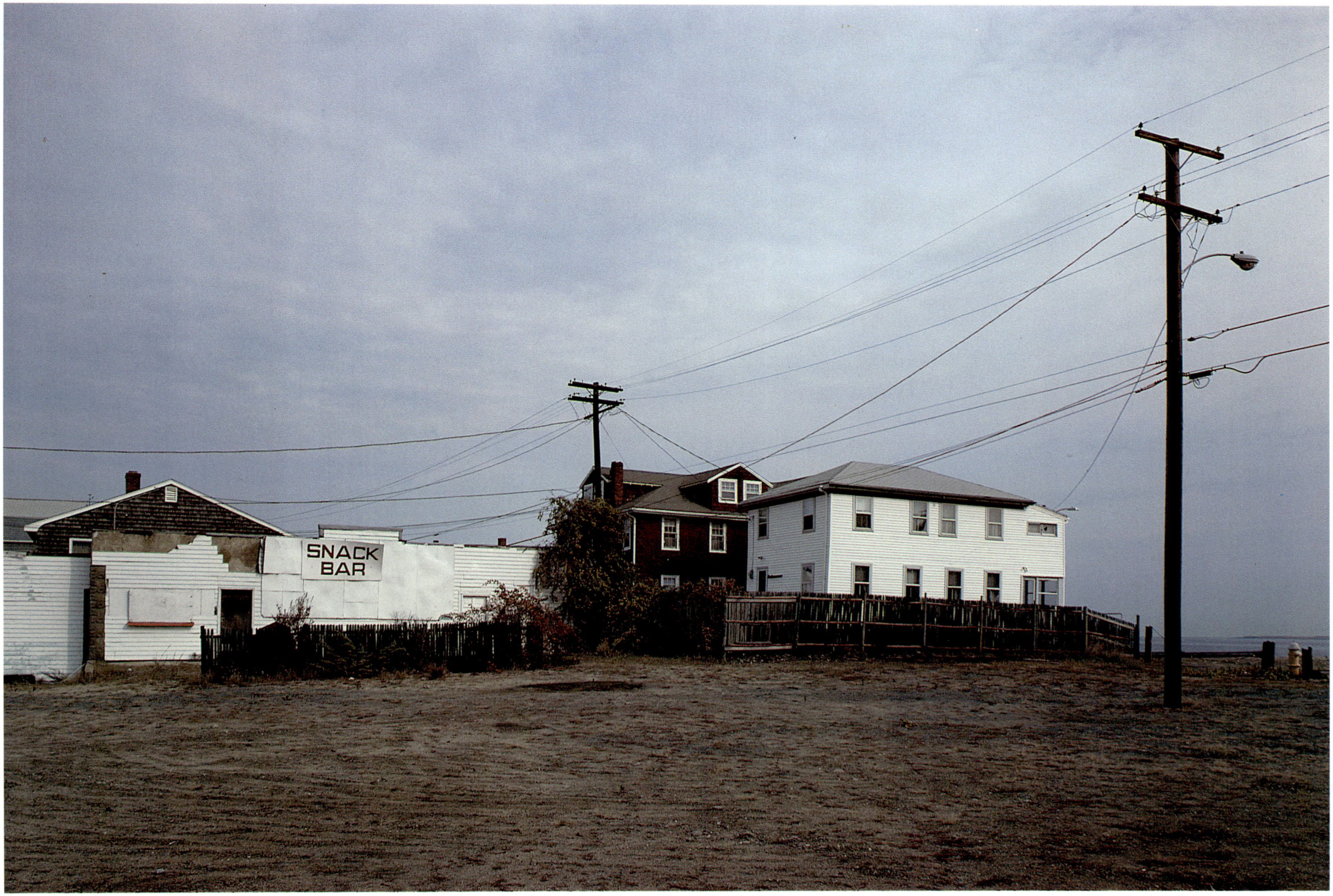
SNACK
BAR

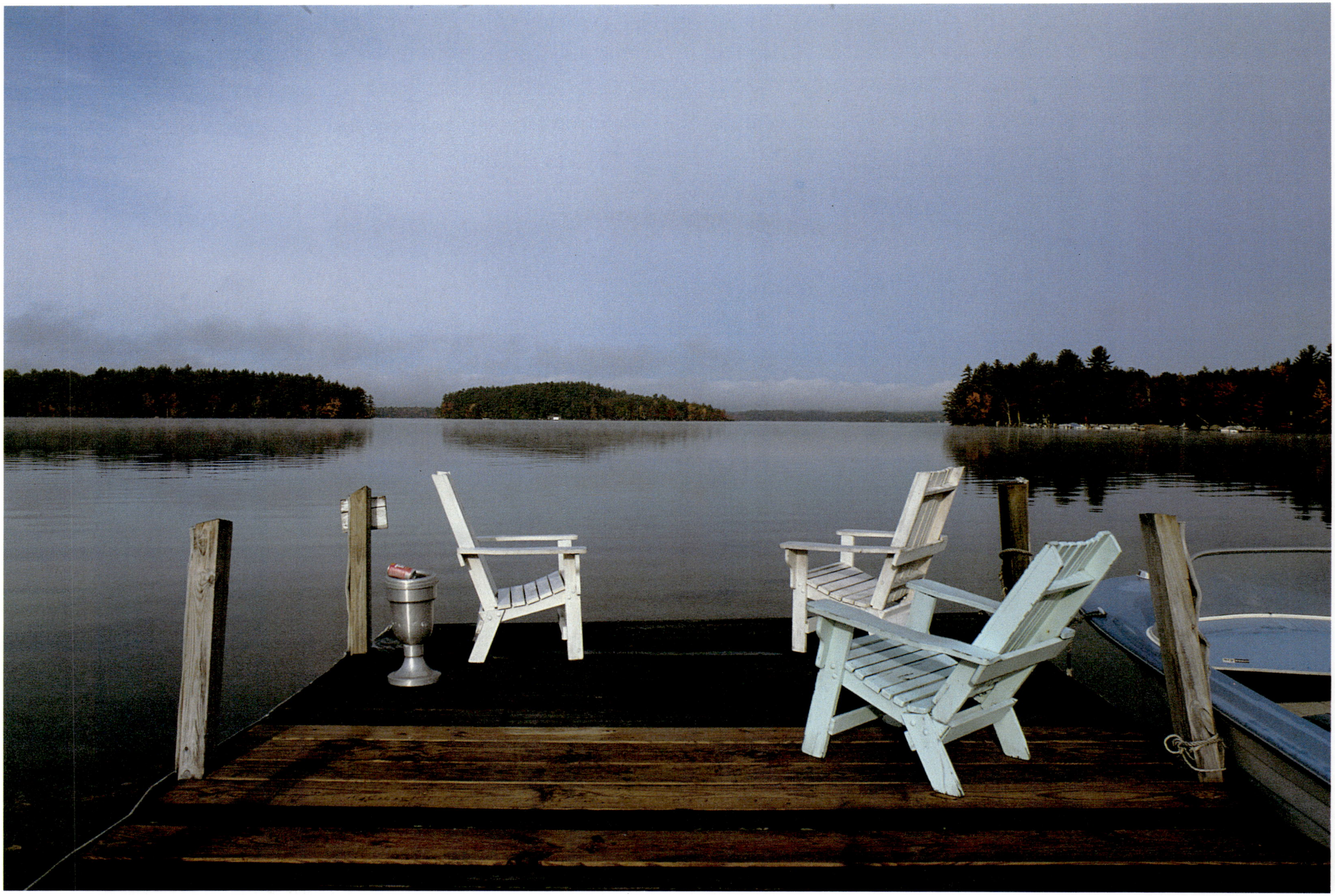

Drink

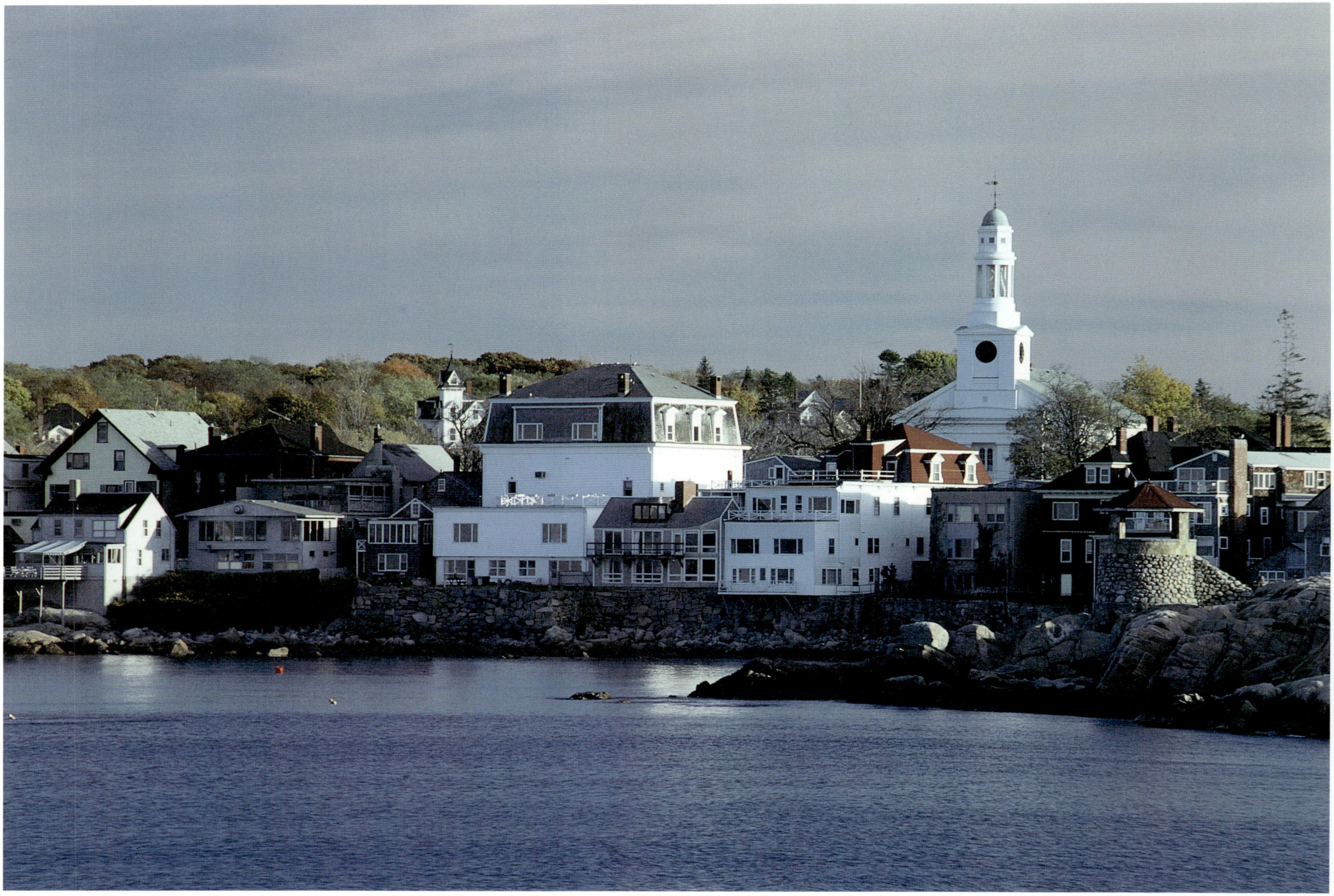

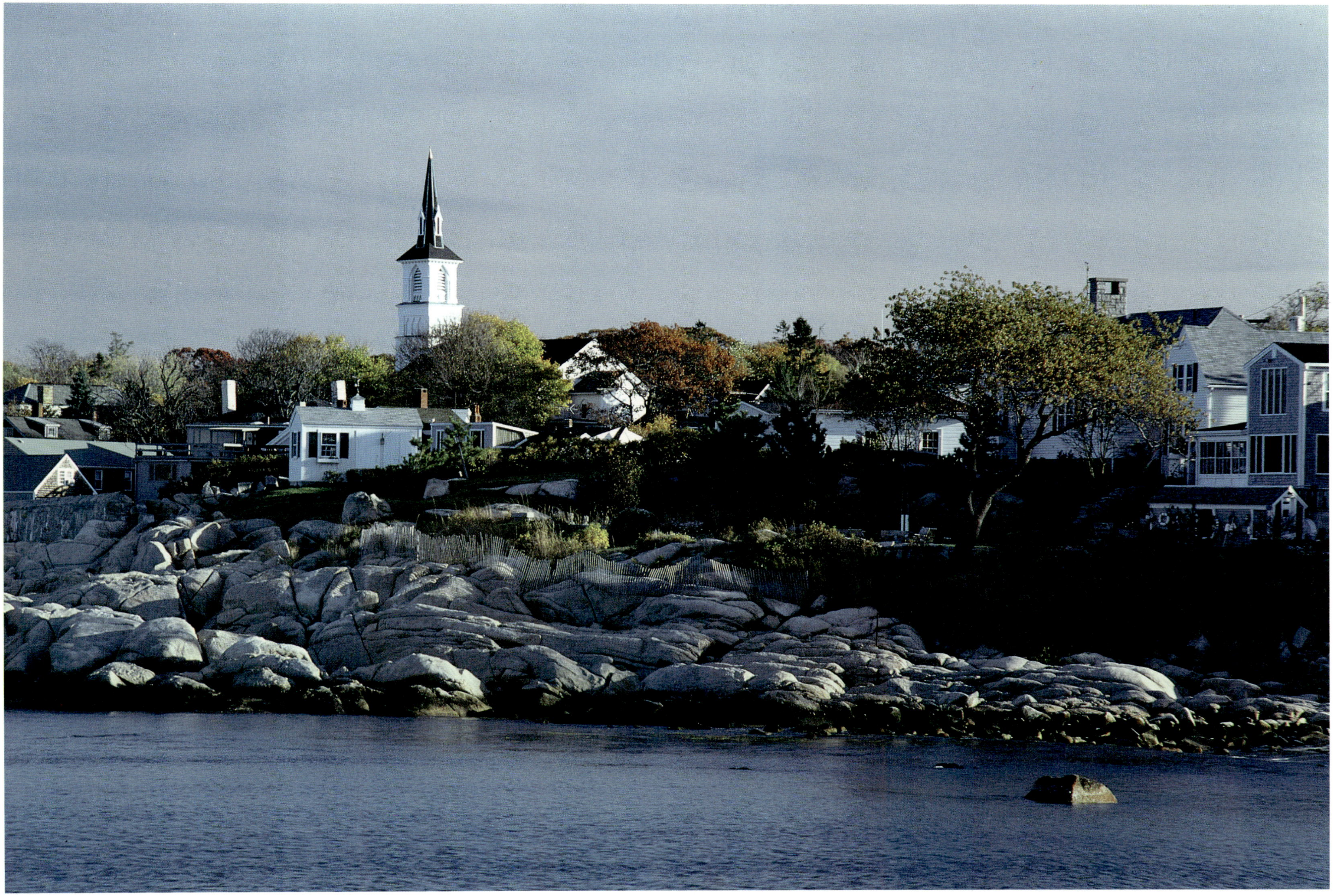

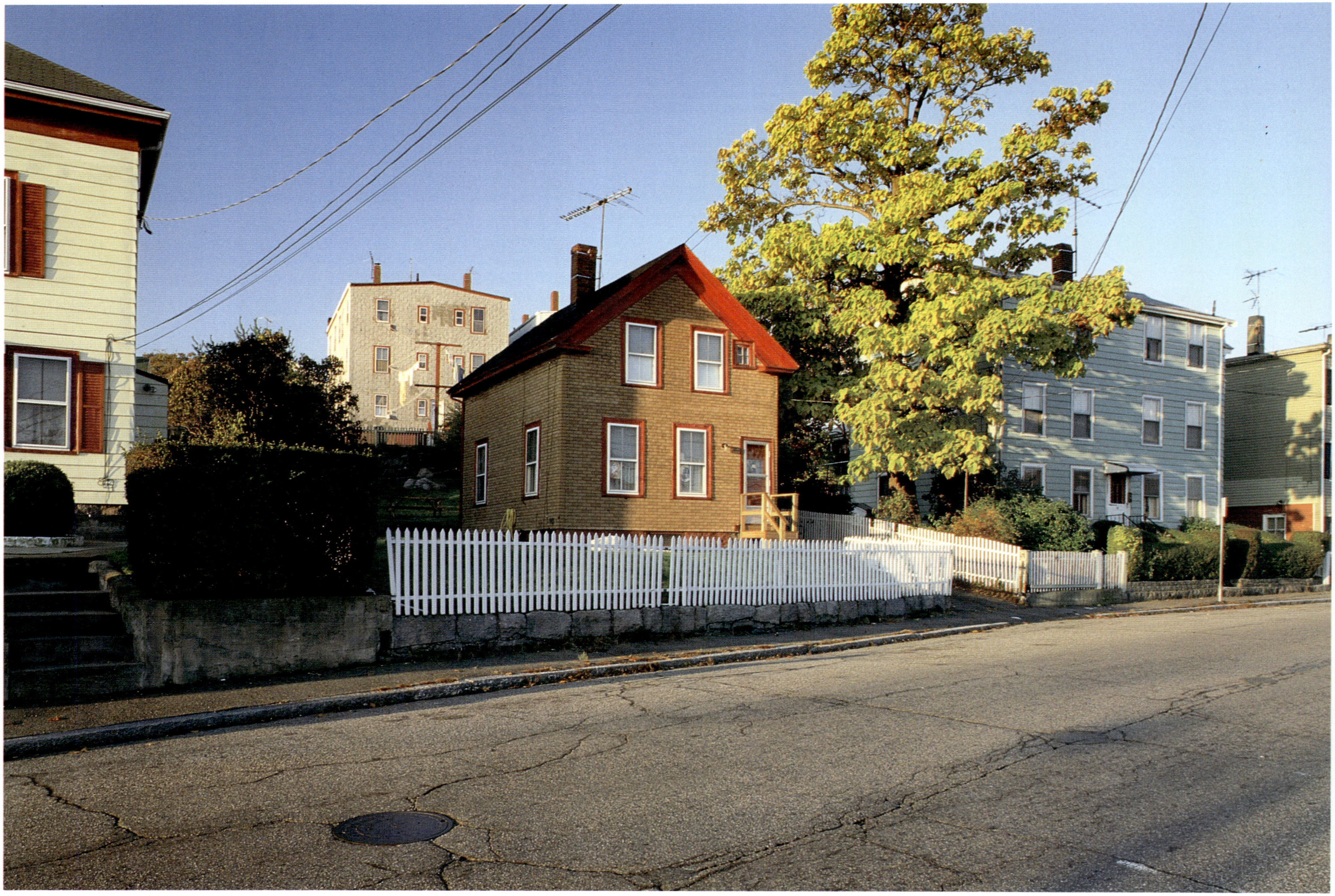

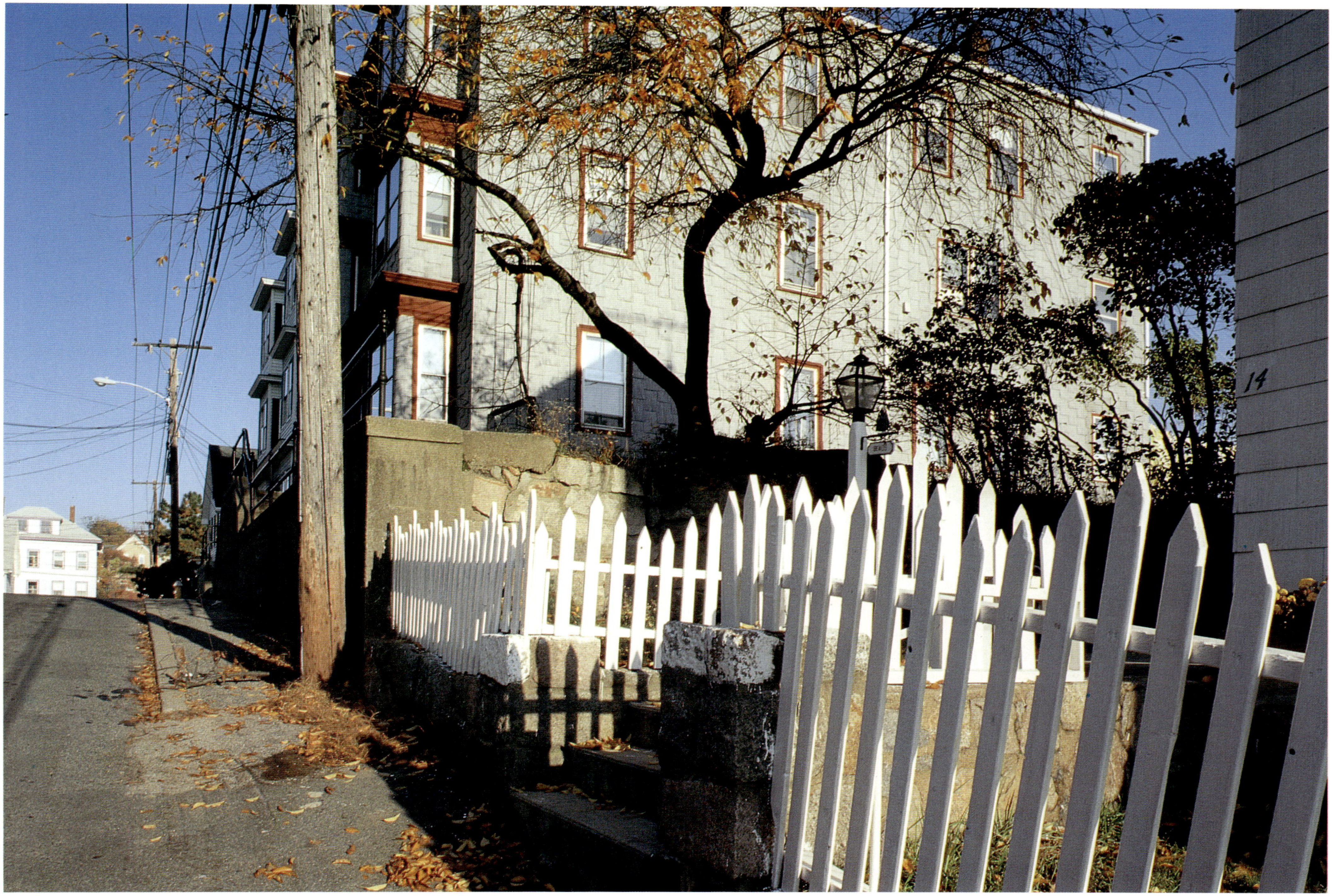
14

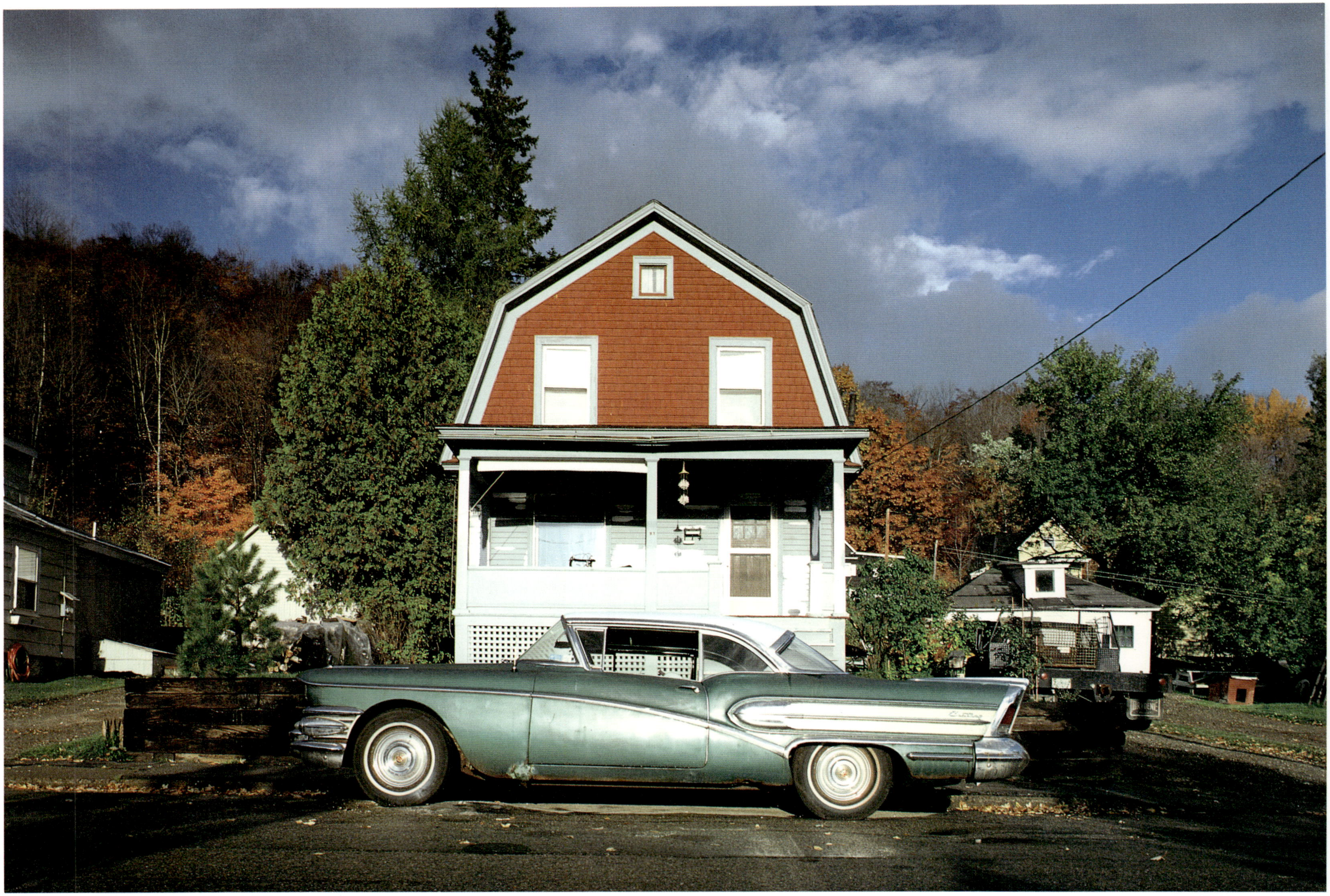

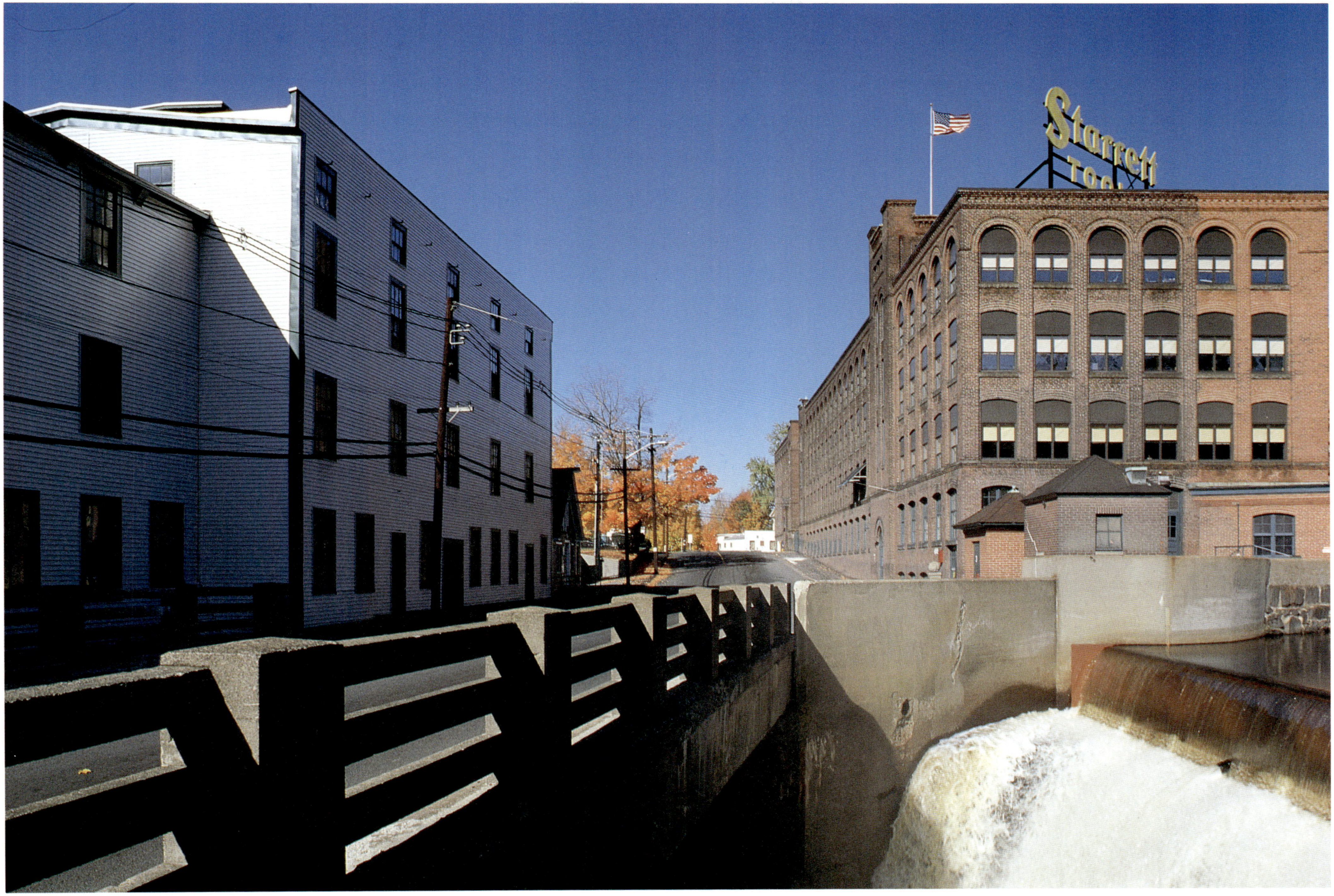
Starrett

52

53

54

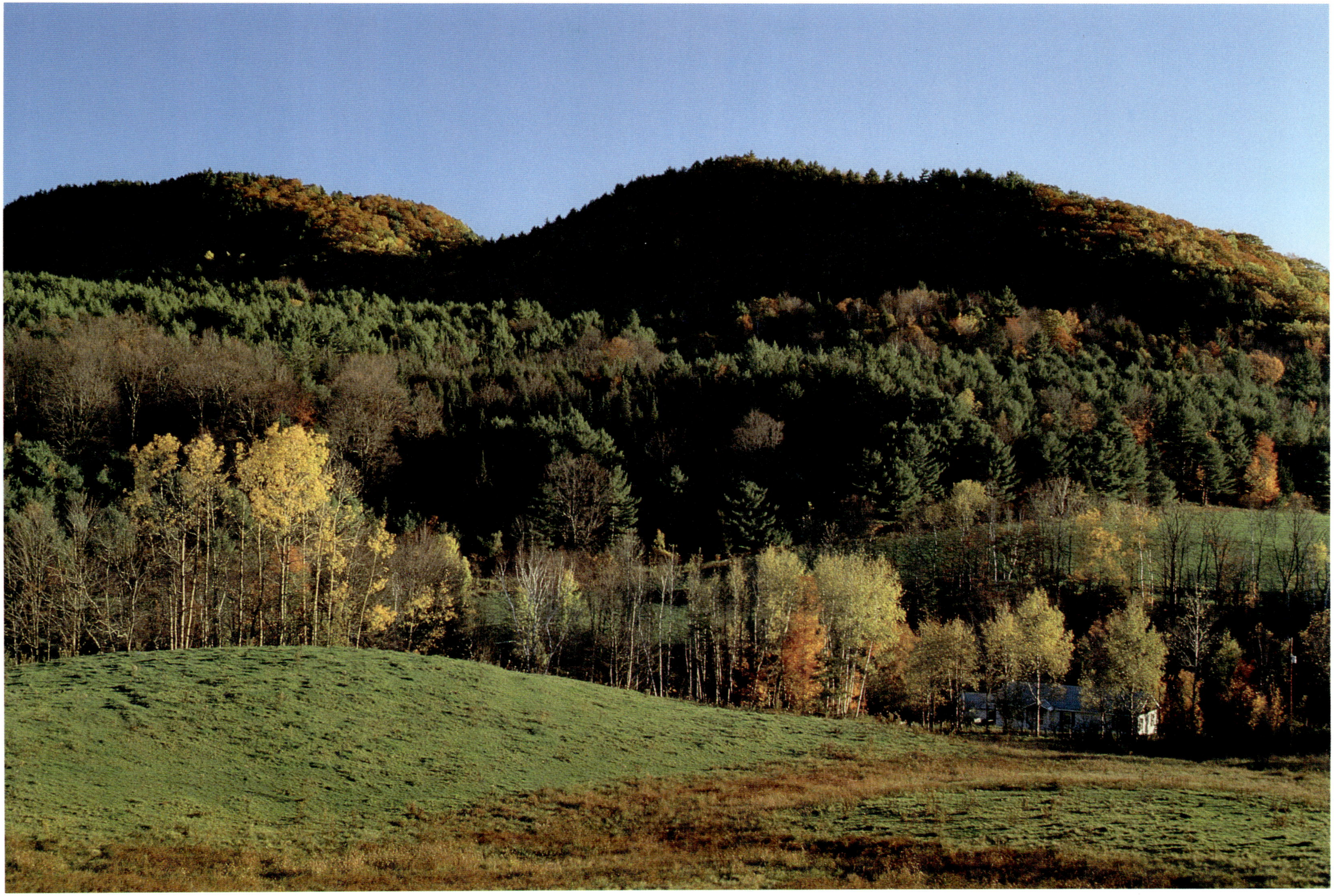

56

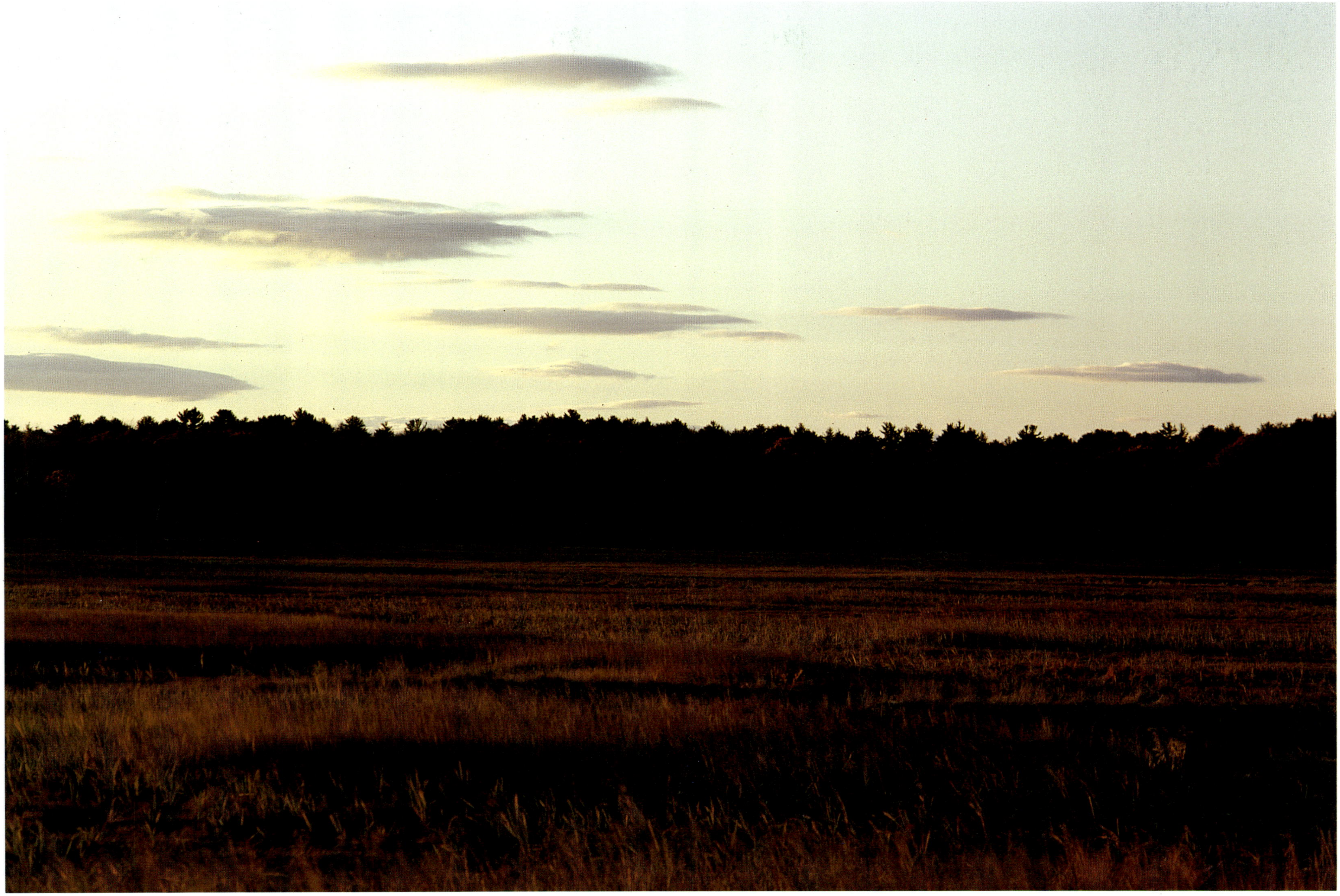

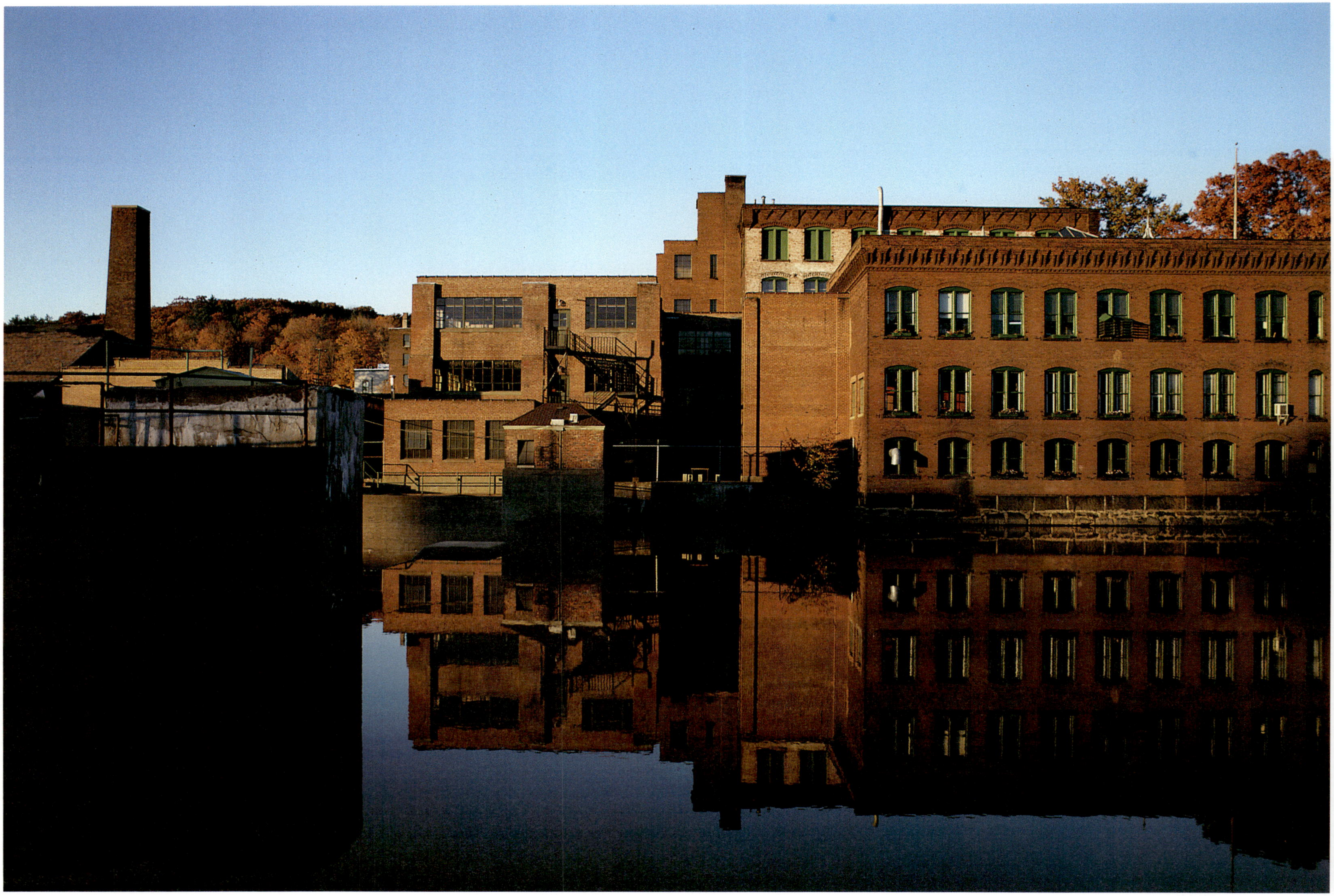

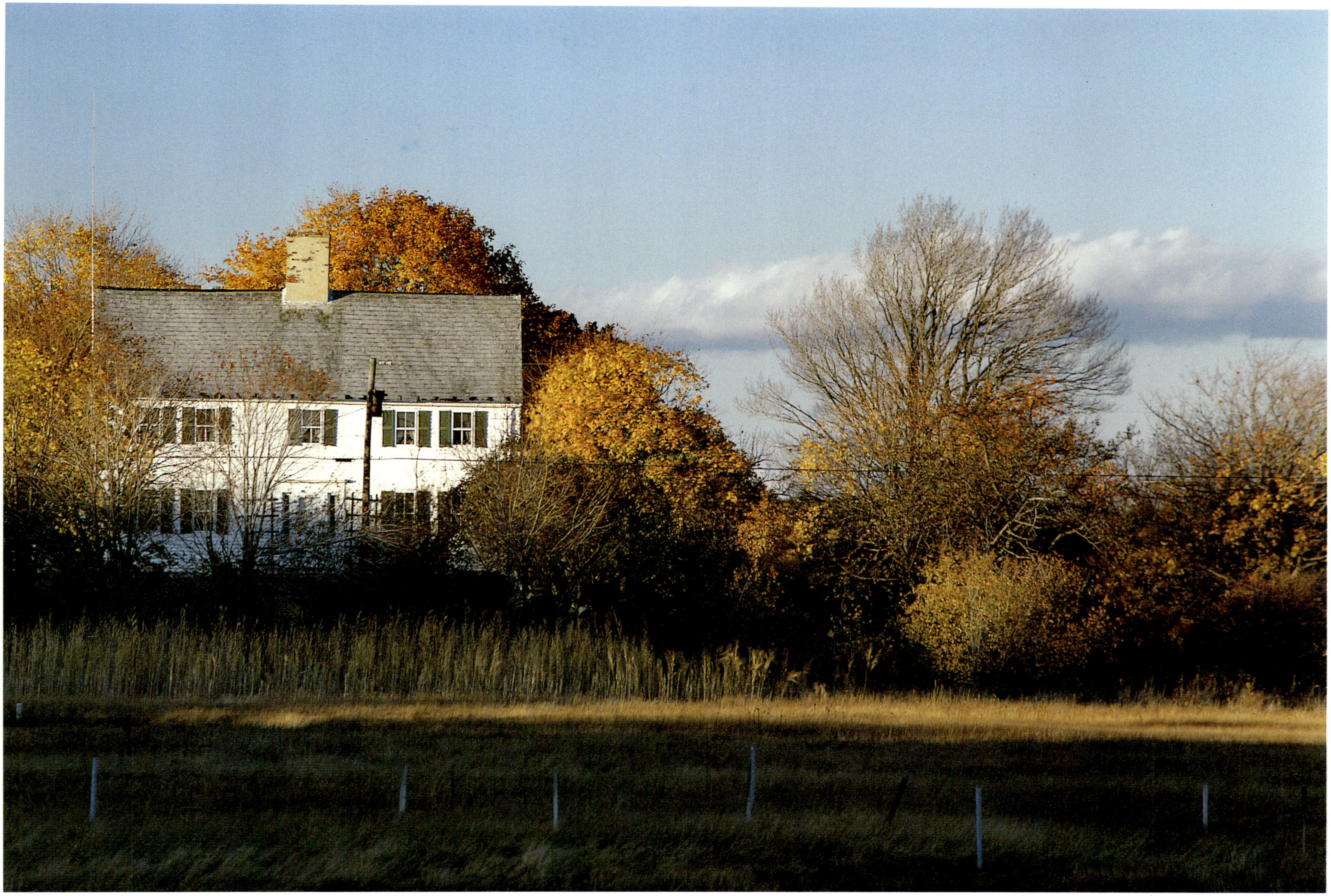

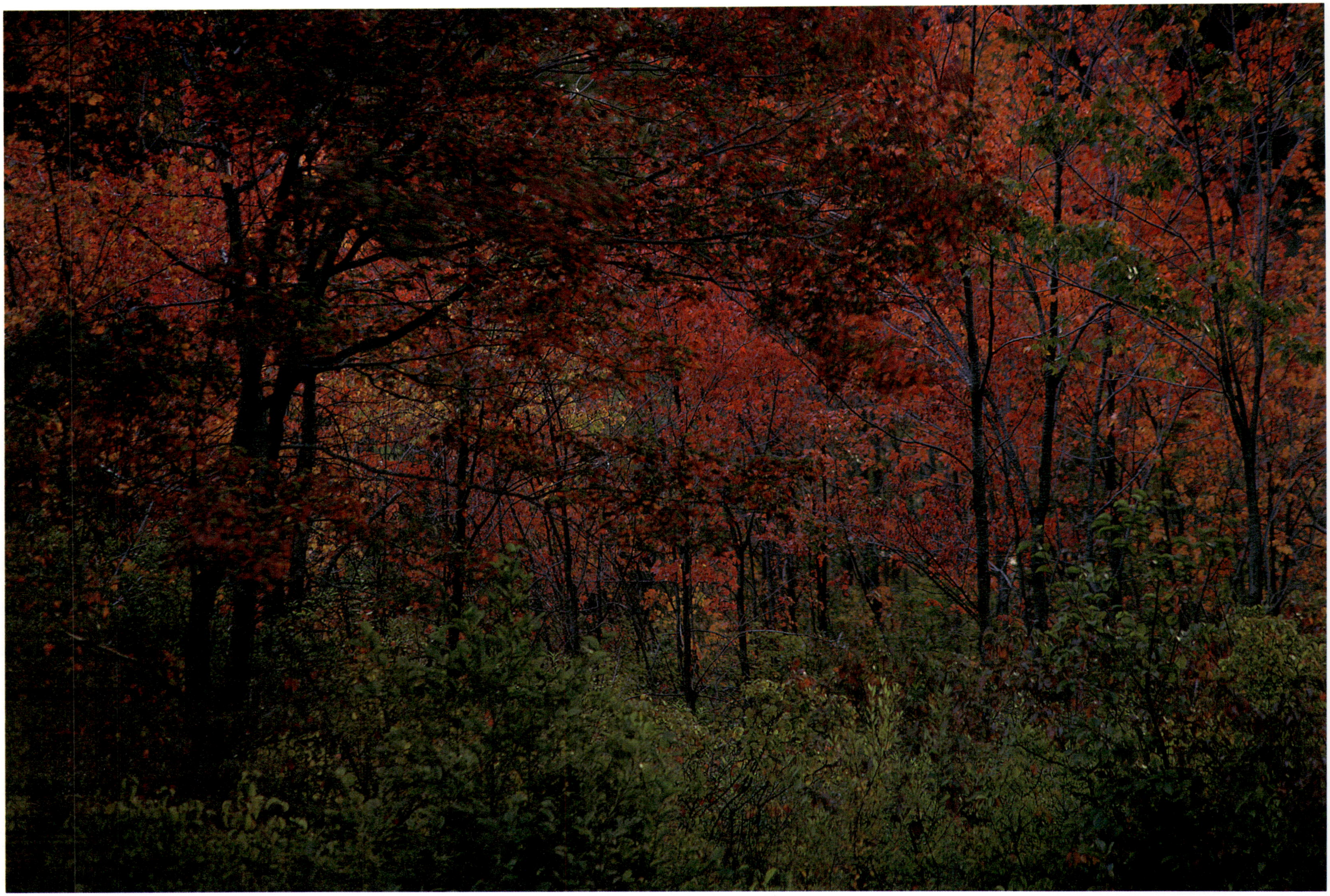

61

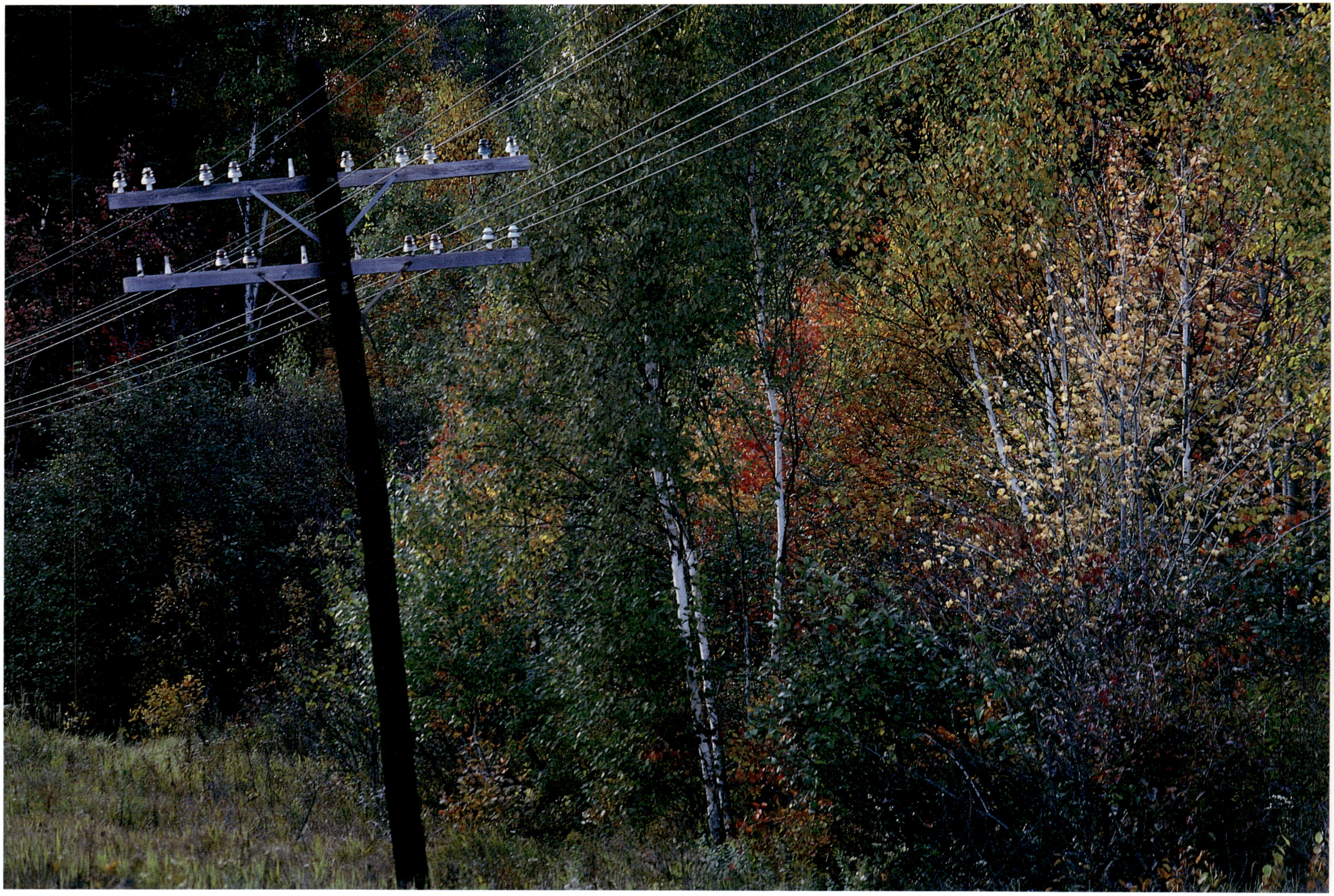

SUNOCO
PACKS
1.16
REGULAR
87.9
NO LEAD
91.9
PREMIUM
129.9
DIESEL
106.9
Winston
KEROSENE
COLD SODA

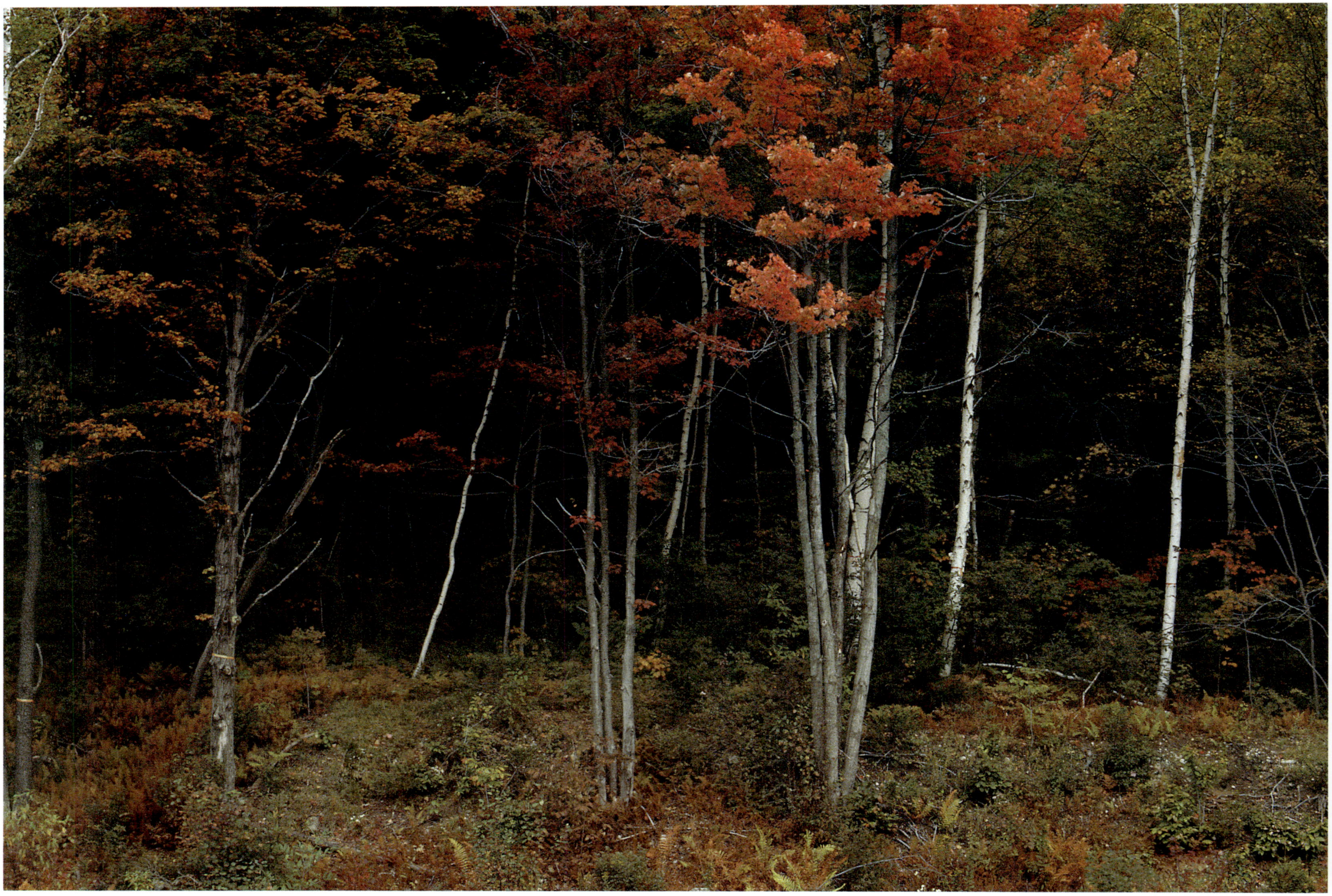

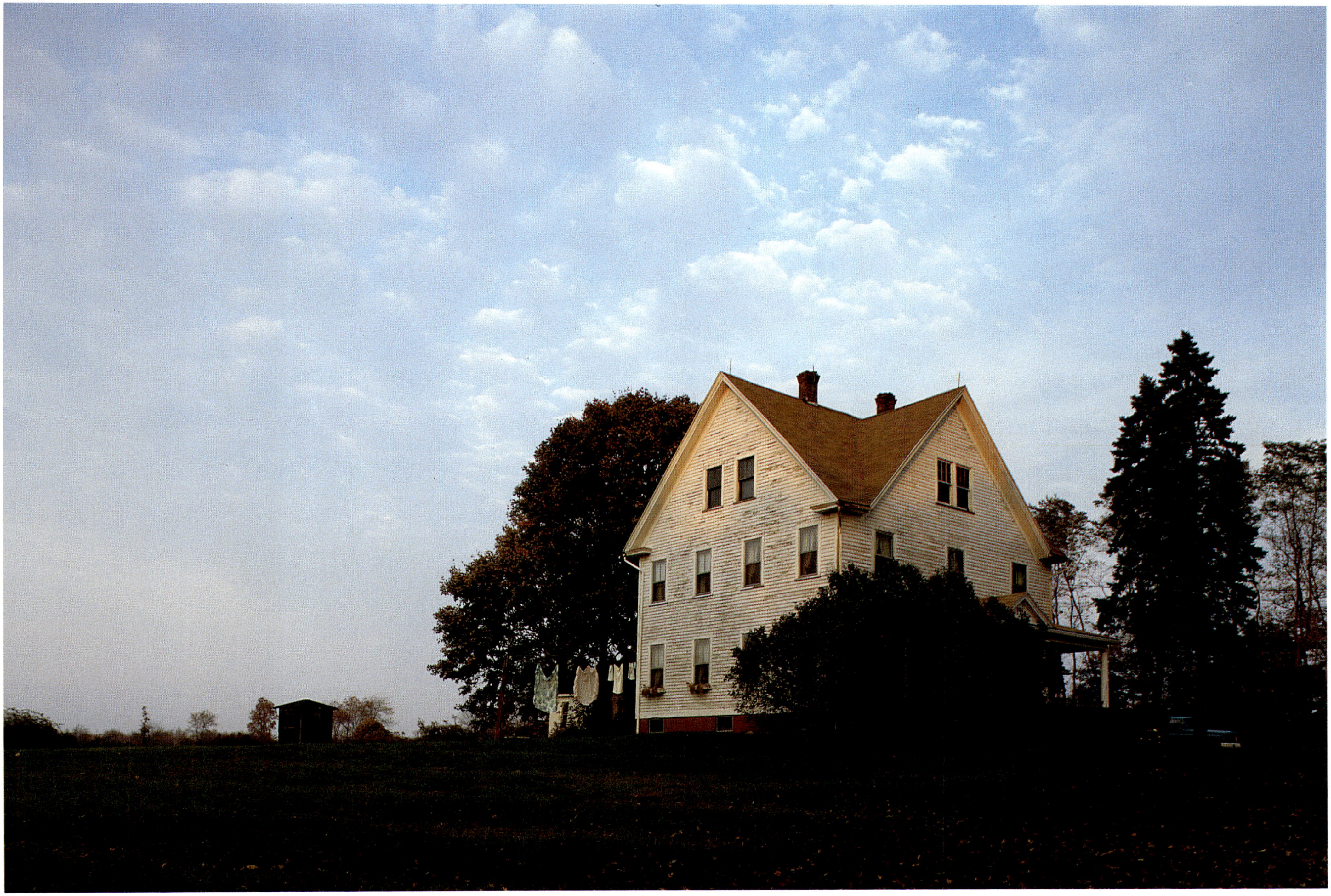

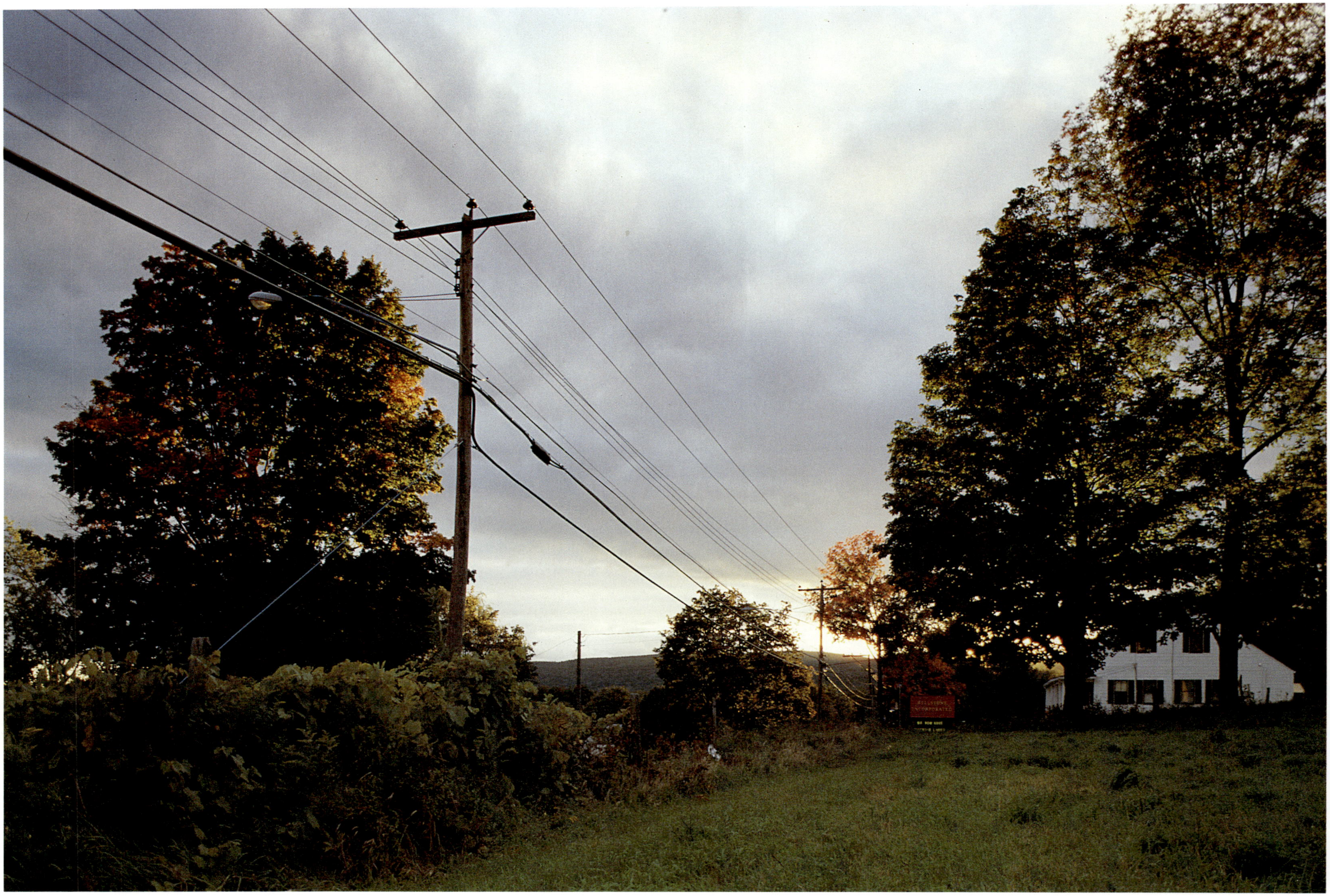

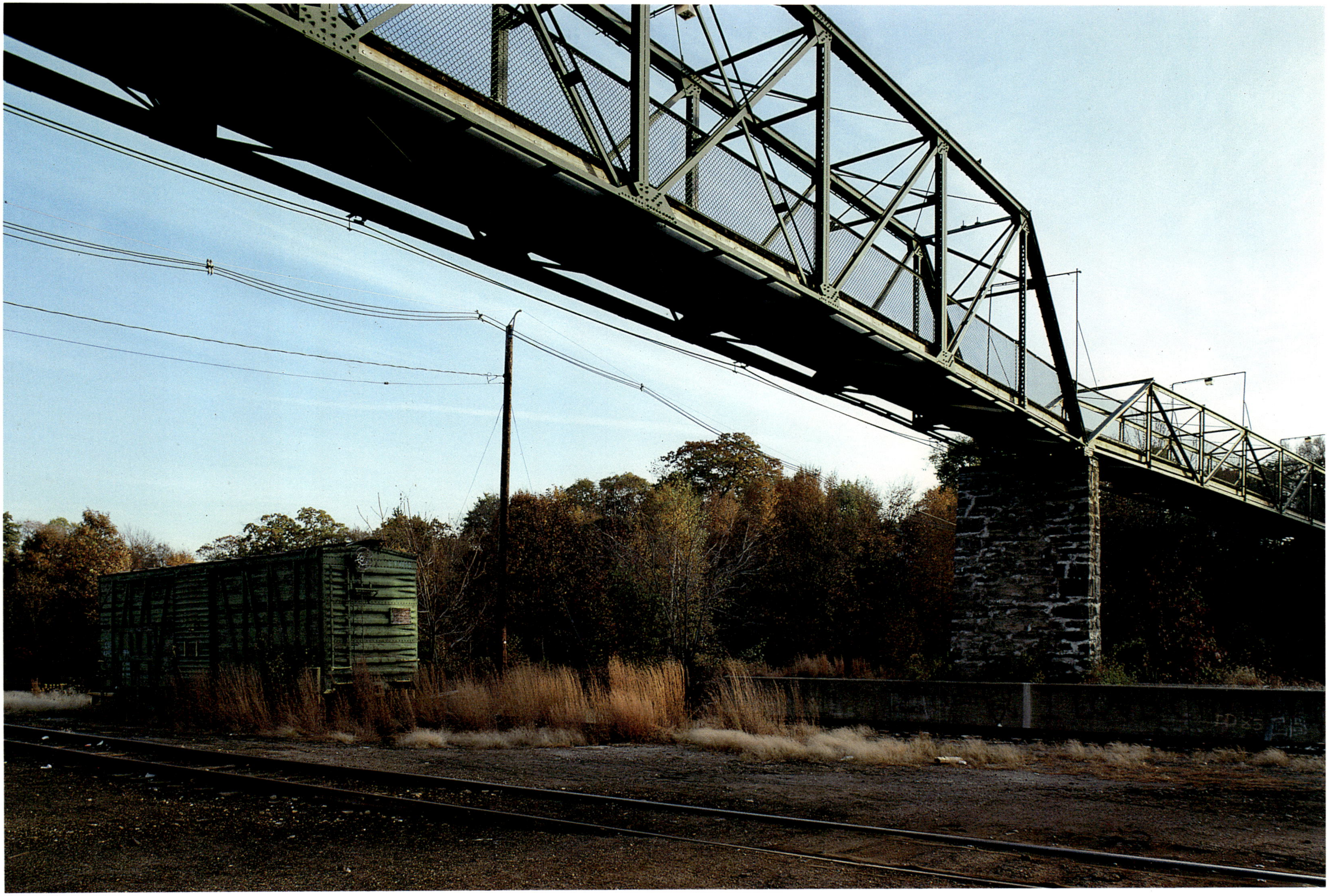

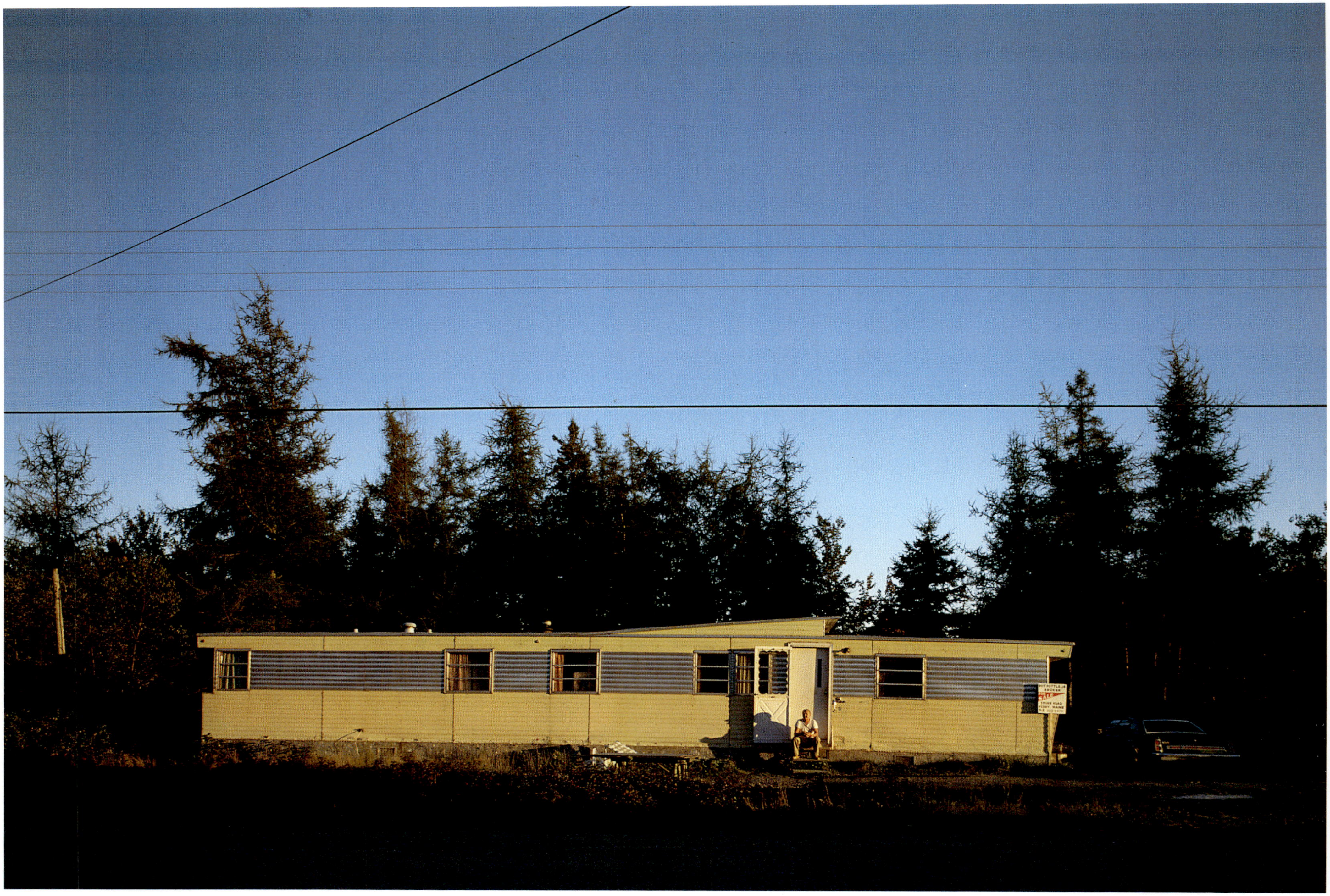

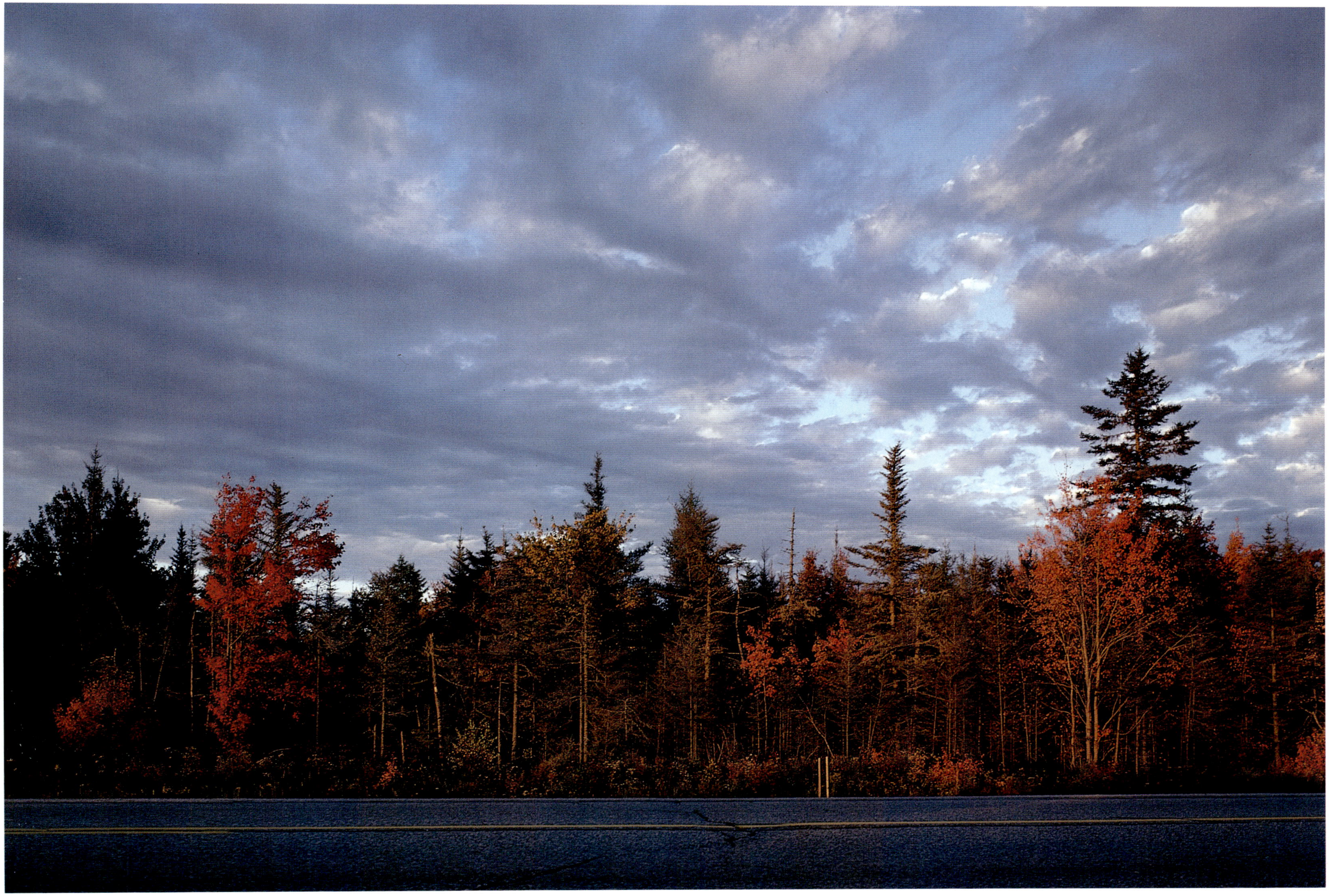

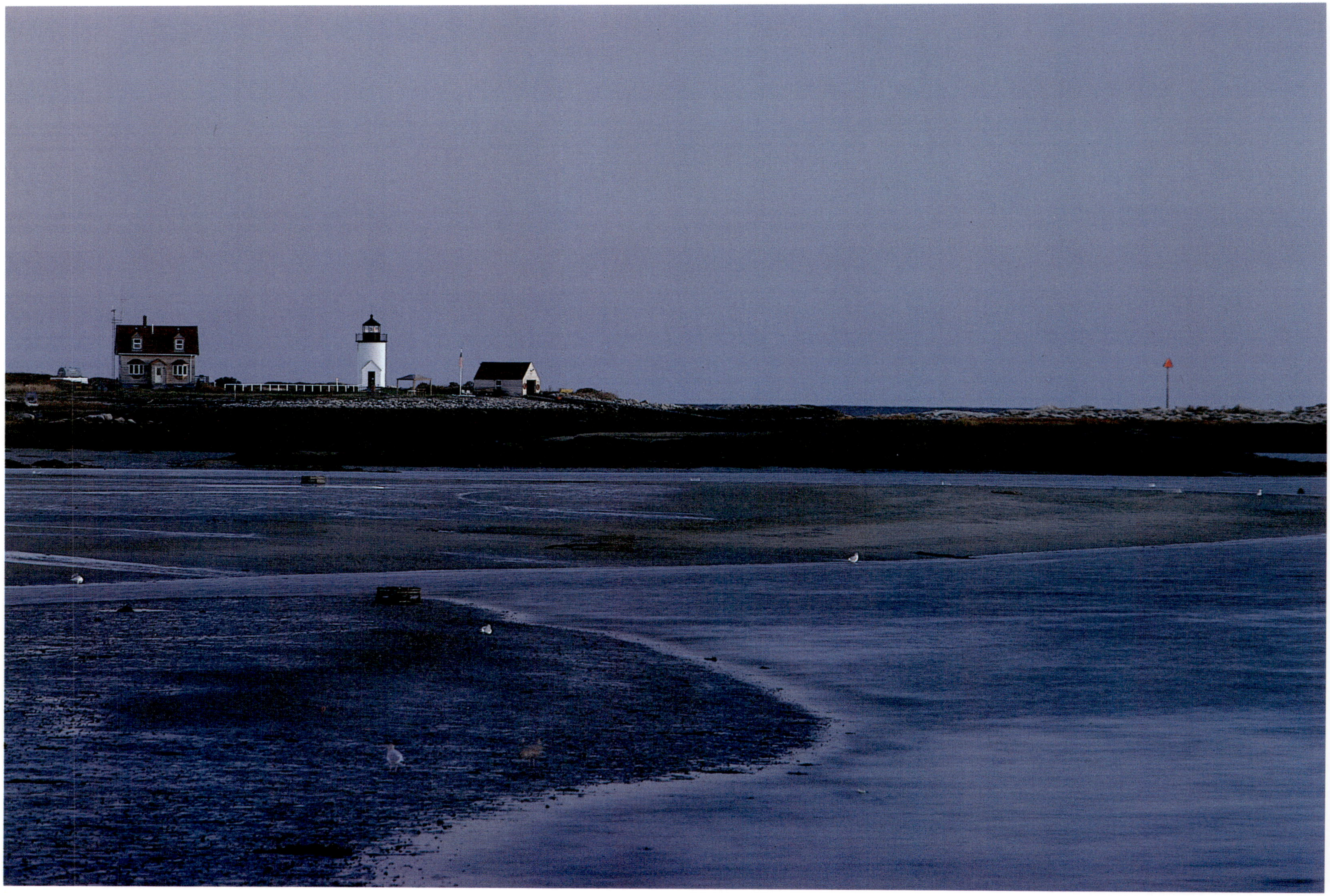

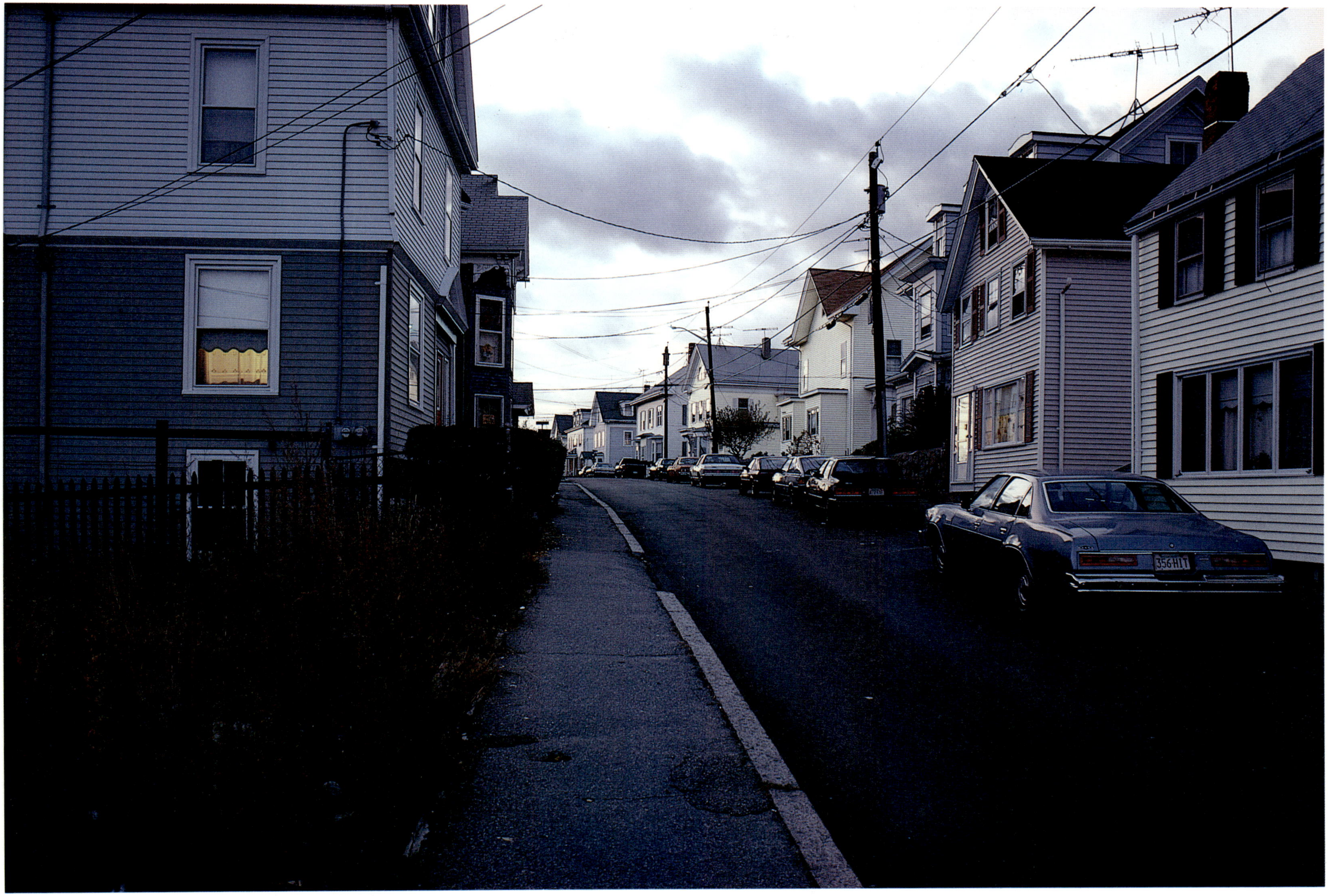
356HIT

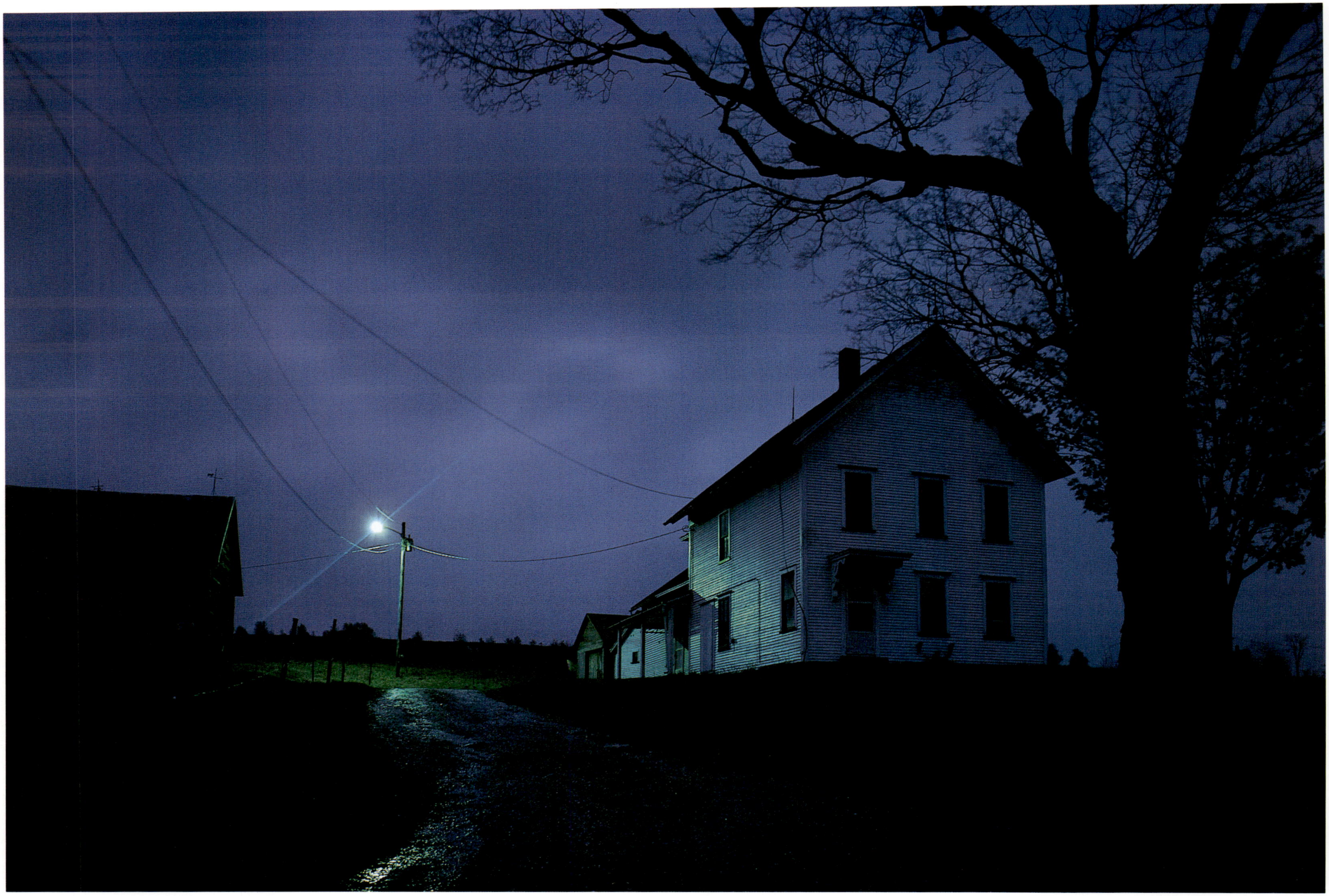

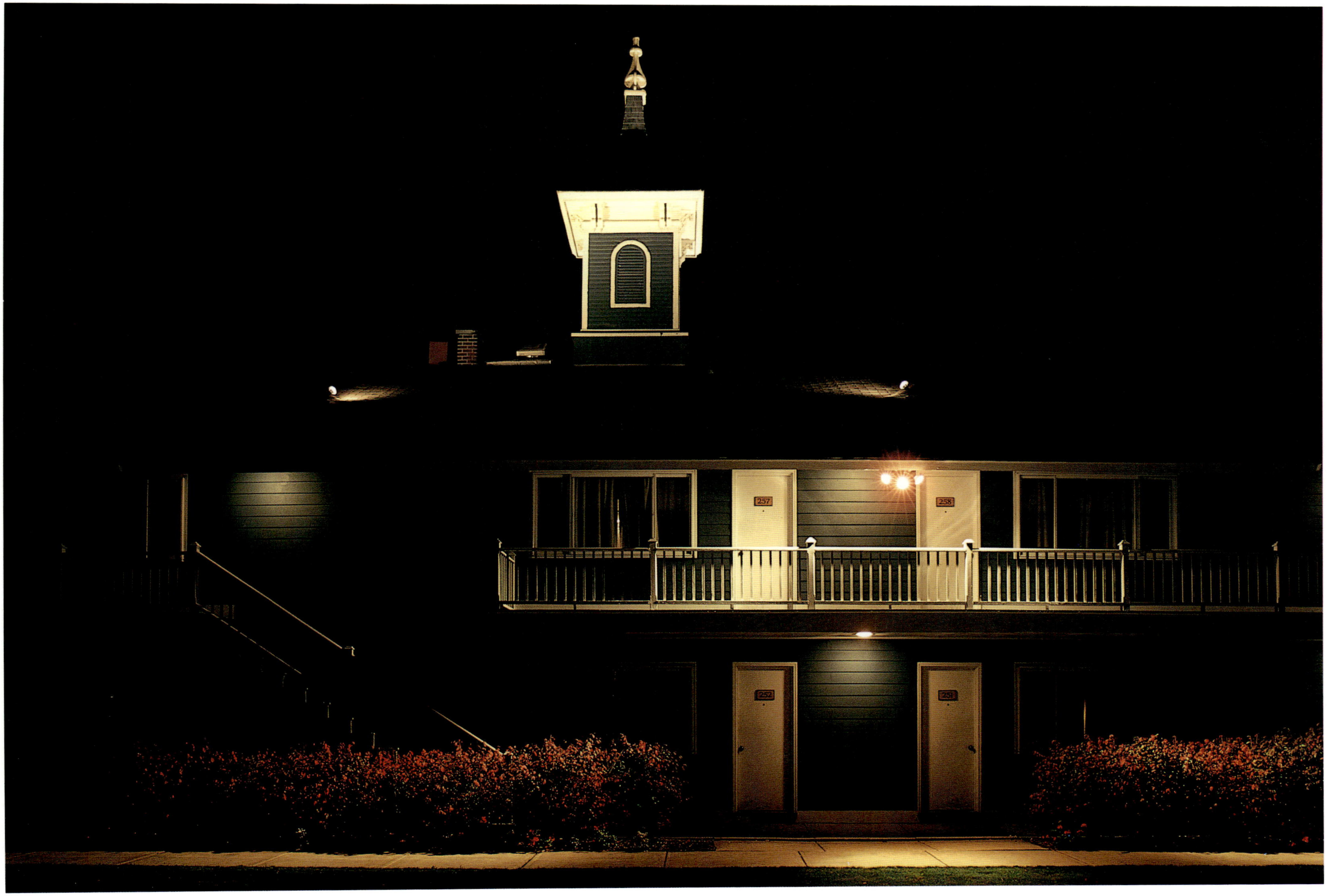

74

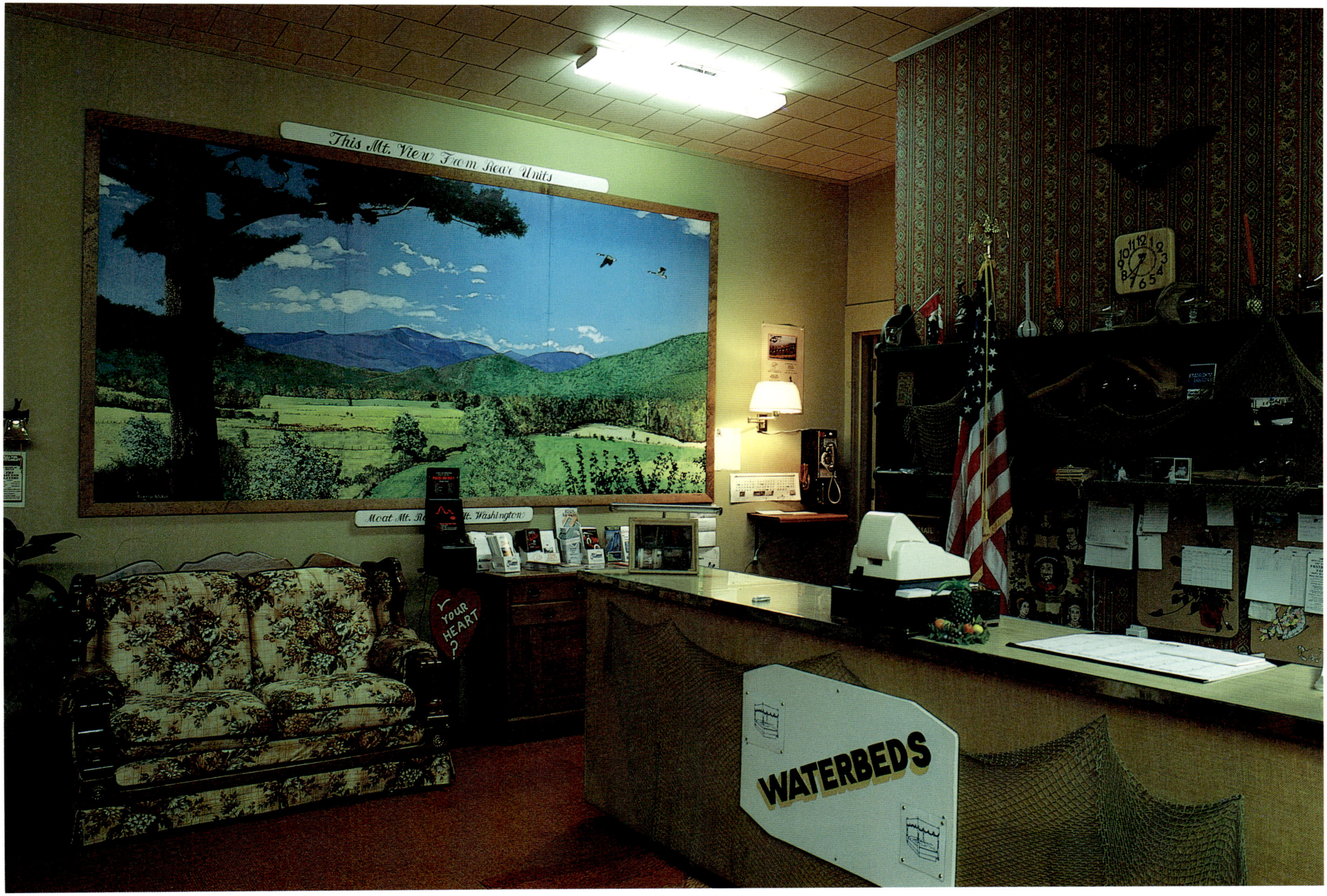
This Mt. View From Rear Units
YOUR HEART?
WATERBEDS

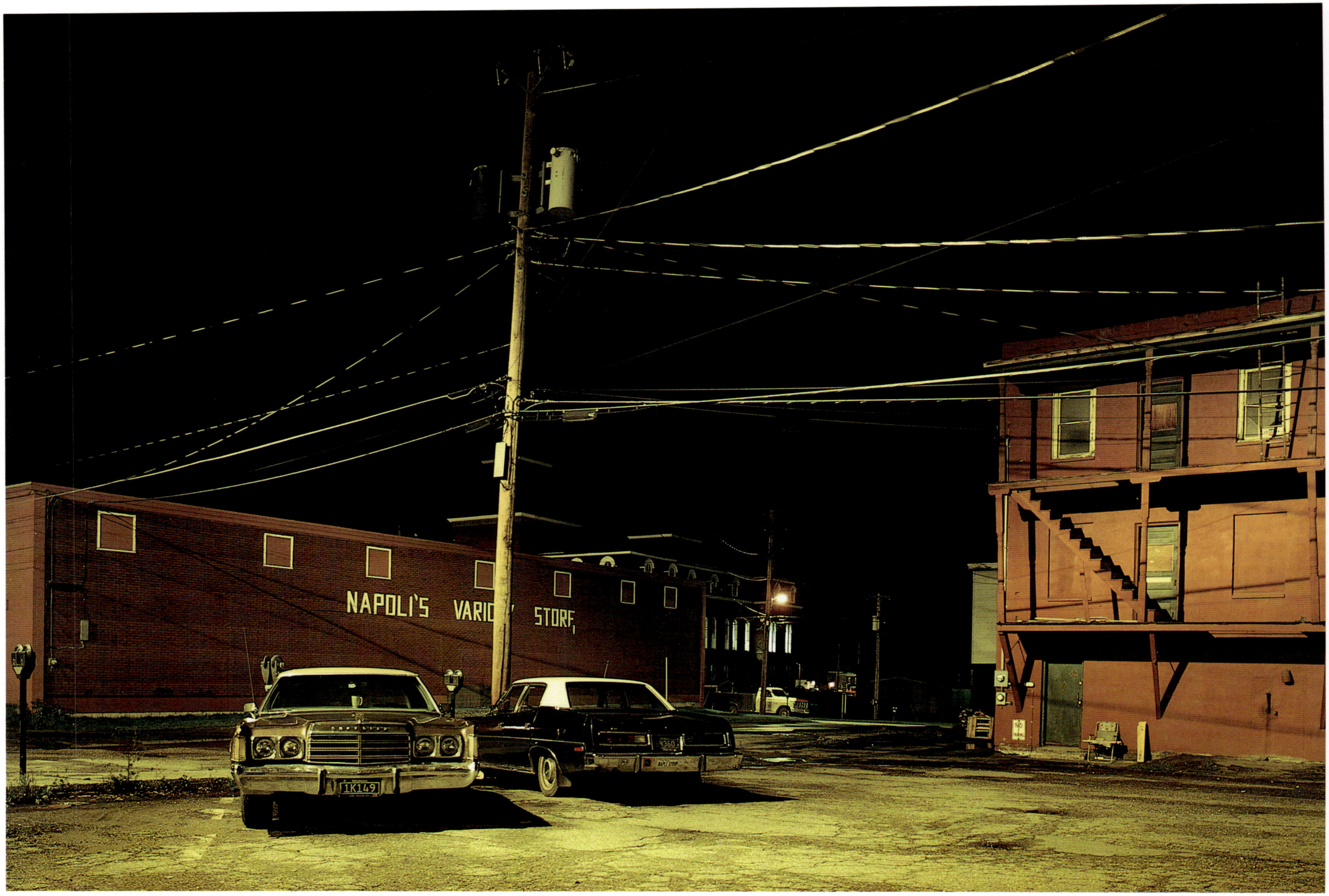
NAPOLI'S
STORE
1K149

77

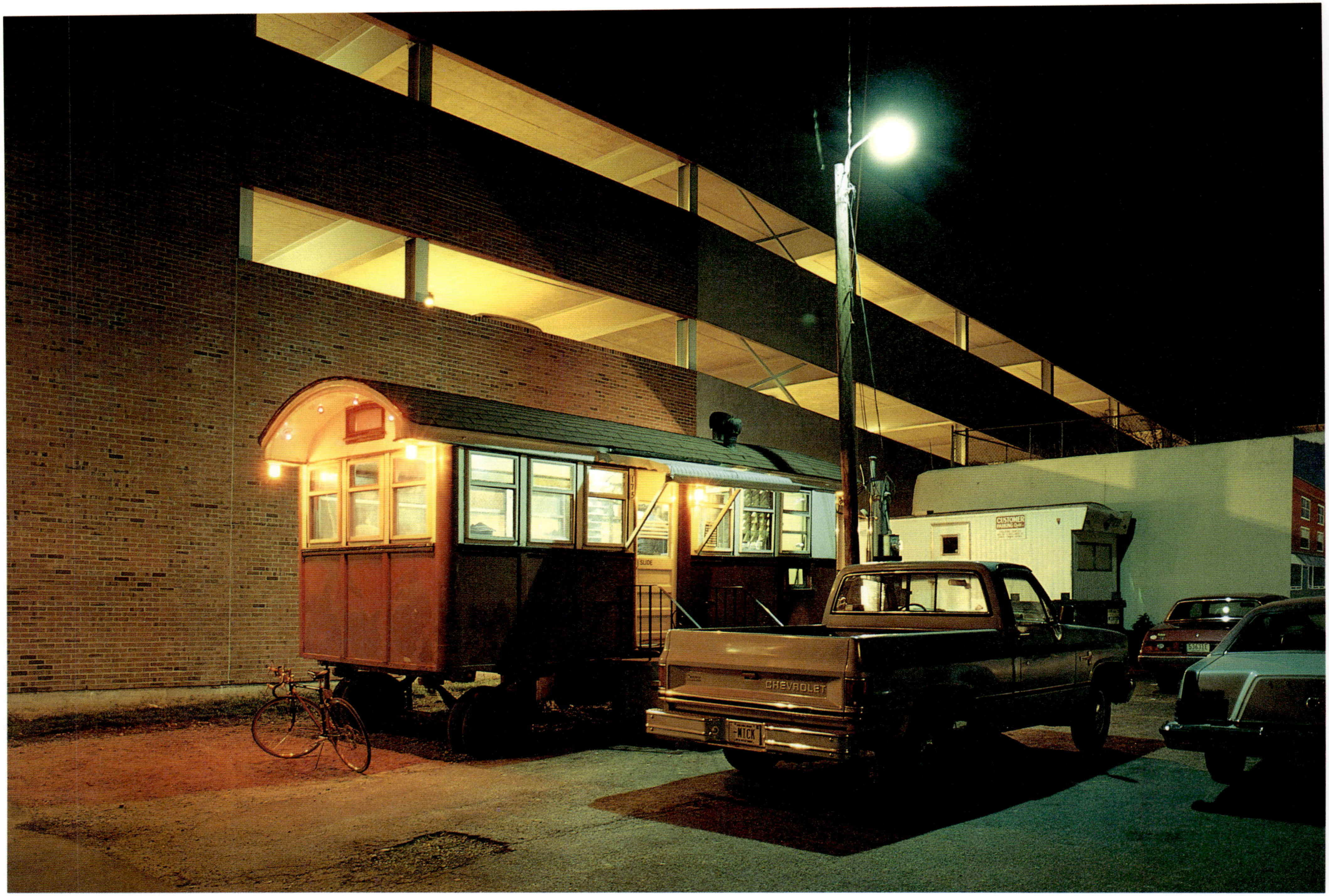
CHEVROLET
CUSTOMER
PARKING Only

79

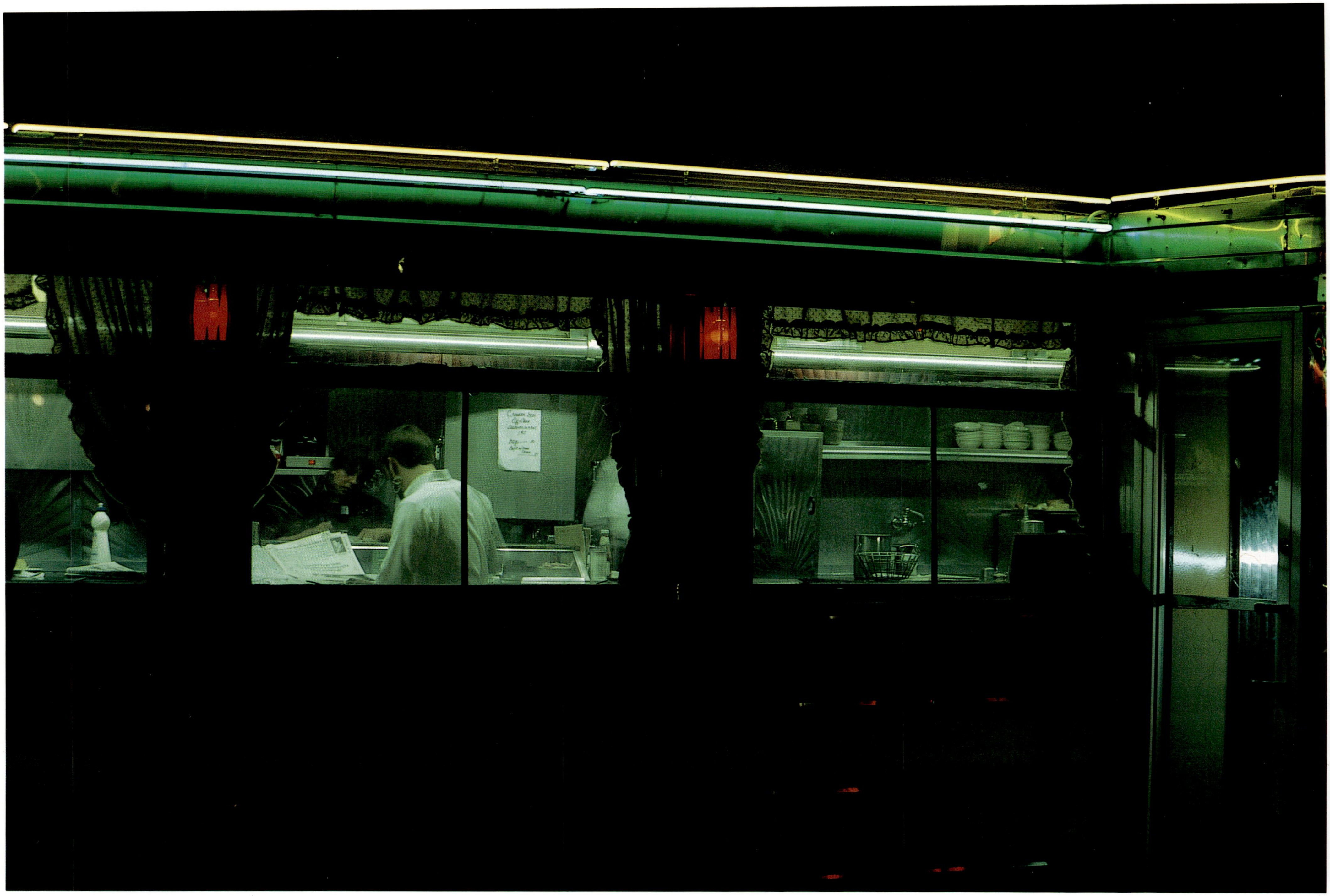